Near to the Heart of God

Crossway books by Sheila Cragg

A WOMAN'S WALK WITH GOD:
A Daily Guide for Prayer & Spiritual Growth

A WOMAN'S JOURNEY TOWARD HOLINESS:
A Daily Guide for Prayer & Godly Living

A WOMAN'S PILGRIMAGE OF FAITH:
A Daily Guide for Prayer & Spiritual Maturity

A SCRIPTURE PRAYER JOURNAL

NEAR
to the
HEART
of
GOD

COMPILED BY

Sheila Cragg

CROSSWAY BOOKS ❦ WHEATON, ILLINOIS
A DIVISION OF GOOD NEWS PUBLISHERS

Near to the Heart of God
Copyright © 2000 by Sheila Cragg
Published by Crossway Books, a division of Good News Publishers
1300 Crescent Street, Wheaton, Illinois 60187

Cover design and art direction: Cindy Kiple
First printing 2000
Printed in the United States of America

Most Scripture in the prayers in this book is paraphrased from the versions listed below. Scripture quoted directly is handled as follows:

Library of Congress Cataloging-in-Publication Data
Near to the heart of God : a scripture prayer journal /
compiled by Sheila Cragg.
   p.   cm.
   Includes indexes.
   ISBN 1-58134-226-8
   1. Devotional calendars. 2. Spiritual journals—Authorship.
I. Cragg, Sheila, 1938–.
BV4811.N43 2000
242'.2—dc21   00-009200
                                                         CIP

16 15 14 13 12 11 10 09 08 07 06 05 04 03 02 01 00
16 15 14 13 12 11 10 9 8 7 6 5 4 3 2 1

For

Lila Bishop,

Sidney Allen,

Judie Frank,

and

Shirlee Hickey

CONTENTS

INTRODUCTION

*D*o you long for a more meaningful prayer life? Do you often feel at a loss to know how to express your heartfelt concerns to the Lord? In this Scripture prayer journal, you will find the words you need to talk to the Lord and to draw near to His heart in His Word. The daily personalized Scripture prayers will help you present your requests to the Lord, confess sin, express your deepest needs, find comfort, worship the Lord, and offer praises and thanksgiving. Prayers for New Year's, Easter, Thanksgiving, Christmas, and for various other themes are also included.

This devotional journal provides lined spaces for you to record "Praises, Prayers, and Personal Notes." Feel free to write the thoughts and requests that are on your heart even when they don't match the theme of the prayer for that day. Like Scripture itself, on some days the prayers will speak to your need while others won't seem to fit at all. At another time the prayer may be exactly what you needed. As you pray, listen for what the Lord desires to say to you. Then write how the Lord spoke to your heart or helped you express your desires through the Scripture prayer.

This is a private prayer journal, one for yourself alone. If you feel uncomfortable writing detailed requests, you may want to write one word or a brief phrase, or use an initial for the name of the person for whom you are interceding. When you write abbreviated requests, make sure to use an easy clue that will help you remember what you desire to pray about. Some prayers are specifically worded to express intercession for others, with blanks to fill in the name of the person(s) for whom you are praying.

Though our prayers are not always answered the way we desire, we can be assured that the Lord deeply loves us, cares about our heartfelt needs, and is always present with us to comfort and support us. We have this confidence that Jesus "is at the right hand of God . . . interceding for us" (Rom. 8:34).

"In the same way, the Spirit helps us in our weakness. We do not know what we ought to pray for, but the Spirit himself intercedes for us with groans that words cannot express. And he who searches our hearts knows the mind of the Spirit, because the Spirit intercedes for the saints in accordance with God's will" (Rom. 8:26-27).

Regularly go back and pray the requests in your journal. Be sure to record answered prayers with the date near the request, including your praises and perhaps an explanation as to how the answer came about. You'll be surprised and blessed afresh by how God has answered. You'll be reminded of the ways God has led you safely through trials you had long forgotten about. You'll be encouraged and strengthened by His never-failing presence in your life—and you'll be adding more praises!

As you use this book, may you indeed find a place where Jesus, your blessed Redeemer sent from the heart of God, holds you near to the heart of His Father.

Near to the Heart of God

As this new year begins, I will draw near to Your heart, O God, with a true heart in full assurance of faith. Teach me to number my days that I may apply my heart to wisdom. Yes, Lord, I will get wisdom and understanding; I will not forget nor turn away from Your words. I will trust in You with all my heart rather than lean on my own understanding. In all my ways I will acknowledge You and trust You to direct my paths. Now may the words of my mouth and the meditations of my heart be acceptable in Your sight, O Lord, my strength and my redeemer.

PRAYERS, PRAISES, AND PERSONAL NOTES

_____

_____

_____

_____

_____

_____

Heb. 10:22a; Ps. 90:12; Prov. 4:5; 3:5-6; Ps. 19:14, all KJV paraphrased

Crown This Year with Goodness

Crown this new year with Your goodness, Lord. Be mindful of us, O Lord, bless us; bless our house. Bless those who fear You, both small and great. All Your works shall praise You, Lord, and Your saints shall bless You. Every day I will bless You; and I will praise Your name forever and ever. Seven times a day I will praise You because of Your righteous judgments. I will praise You, O Lord, with my whole heart. At all times throughout this new year, I will continually praise You. I praise You, Lord. Praise the Lord, O my soul.

🍃 PRAYERS, PRAISES, AND PERSONAL NOTES 🍃

_____

_____

_____

_____

_____

_____

_____

Ps. 65:11a; 115:12a, 13; 145:10, 2; 119:164; 9:1a; 34:1; 146:1, all KJV paraphrased

A Thousand Years in God's Sight

Everlasting Father, a thousand years in Your sight are but as yesterday when they are past and as a few hours in the night. Behold, God, You are great and beyond understanding; Your years cannot be numbered or searched out. You appointed the moon for seasons; the sun knows its going down. And You change the times and the seasons; You remove and set up kings; You give wisdom to the wise and knowledge to them that have understanding. Therefore, in these times and in this new year, I commit my spirit—my heart and my life—into Your hand; for You have redeemed me, O Lord God of truth. I commit my way to You, Lord; I also trust in You.

PRAYERS, PRAISES, AND PERSONAL NOTES

_____

_____

_____

_____

_____

Ps. 90:4; Job 36:26; Ps. 104:19; Dan. 2:21; Ps. 31:5; Ps. 37:5a, all KJV paraphrased

Teach Me to Revere You

Father God, in this new year, I will come and listen to You; for You will teach me to revere and worshipfully fear You. I desire life and long for many days that I may see good. Therefore, I will keep my tongue from evil and my lips from speaking deceit. I will keep my heart from idols. I will be careful so that my heart will not be enticed to turn away and worship other gods and bow down to them. I will submit to You, O Lord, and be at peace; thereby good will come to me. I will receive the law from Your mouth and lay up Your words in my heart. For then I will delight in You, Almighty One, and will lift up my face to You, O God.

🔥 PRAYERS, PRAISES, AND PERSONAL NOTES 🔥

_____

_____

_____

_____

_____

Ps. 34:11-13 AMP; 1 John 5:21; Deut. 11:16; Job 22:21-22, 26, all paraphrased

God's Good Work

Author and Perfecter of our faith, Your way is perfect; Your Word is flawless. You are a shield for _____ _____ (*names of those for whom you are praying*), and I pray they will take refuge in You throughout this new year. For who is God besides You, Lord? Who is their rock except You? Arm them with strength and make their ways perfect. Encourage them to be confident of this, that You who began a good work in them will carry it on to completion until the day of Christ Jesus. And I pray, O God, that they will stand perfect and complete in all Your will.

PRAYERS, PRAISES, AND PERSONAL NOTES

_____

_____

_____

_____

_____

_____

2 Sam. 22:31-33; Phil. 1:6; Col. 4:12b, all KJV paraphrased

Wholehearted Devotion

O kind and loving Lord, satisfy me in the morning with Your unfailing love, that I may sing for joy and be glad throughout this new year. "Remember, O Lord, your great mercy and love, for they are from of old." "I will remember the deeds of the Lord; yes, I will remember your miracles of long ago. I will meditate on all your works and consider all your mighty deeds." I acknowledge You, O God, and will serve You with wholehearted devotion and with a willing mind, for You search my heart and understand every motive behind my thoughts.

❧ PRAYERS, PRAISES, AND PERSONAL NOTES ❧

_____

_____

_____

_____

_____

_____

_____

Ps. 90:14 paraphrased; Ps. 25:6; 77:11-12 not paraphrased; 1 Chron. 28:9a paraphrased

My Heart Rejoices

How good it is for me to draw near to Your heart, O God, for I have put my trust in You that I may tell of all Your wonderful works. I will sing to You, Lord, because You have dealt bountifully with me. For great is Your loving mercy toward me. I have trusted in Your mercy; my heart rejoices in Your salvation. For Your lovingkindness is before my eyes, and I have walked in Your truth. I have not hid Your righteousness within my heart; I have declared Your faithfulness and Your salvation. I have not concealed Your lovingkindness and Your truth. I praise You, Lord. Throughout this new year I will praise You, Lord, with my whole heart.

❧ PRAYERS, PRAISES, AND PERSONAL NOTES ❧

_____

_____

_____

_____

_____

Ps. 73:28; 13:6; 86:13a; 13:5; 26:3 40:10a; 111:1a, all KJV paraphrased

A New Heart

Jesus, You have been teaching me in regard to my former way of life to put off my old self, which is corrupted by deceitful desires, to be made new in the attitude of my mind and to put on a new self, created to be like You in true righteousness and holiness. Lord, give me a new heart and put a new spirit within me; remove from me a heart of stone and give me a heart of flesh. Fill me with Your Spirit and move me to follow Your decrees and to be careful to keep Your laws. For Your eyes range throughout the earth to strengthen those whose hearts are fully committed to You.

✿ PRAYERS, PRAISES, AND PERSONAL NOTES ✿

_____

_____

_____

_____

_____

_____

Eph. 4:22-24; Ezek. 36:26-27; 2 Chron. 16:9, all paraphrased, A Woman's Walk with God, 36

Create in Me a Clean Heart

I delight to do Your will, O my God: yes, Your law is within my heart. I seek Your favor with my whole heart; be merciful to me according to Your word. Cast me not away from Your presence, and take not Your Holy Spirit from me. Examine me, Lord, and prove me by looking closely into my heart and mind. "Create in me a clean heart, O God; and renew a right spirit within me." Restore to me the joy of Your salvation, and uphold me with Your free spirit.

🌿 PRAYERS, PRAISES, AND PERSONAL NOTES 🌿

_____

_____

_____

_____

_____

_____

_____

_____

Ps. 40:8; 119:58; 51:11; 26:2 paraphrased; Ps. 51:10 not paraphrased; Ps. 51:12 paraphrased, all KJV

Grant Them Wisdom

Lord, I pray that_____
will cry out for insight and understanding. May they search for these as they would for lost money or hidden treasure. Then they will understand what it means to fear You, Lord, and they will gain knowledge of You. For You grant wisdom! From Your mouth come knowledge and understanding. O Lord, You grant a treasure of good sense to the godly. You are their shield, protecting those who walk with integrity. You guard the paths of justice and protect those who are faithful to You.

PRAYERS, PRAISES, AND PERSONAL NOTES

_____

_____

_____

_____

_____

_____

_____

Prov. 2:3-8 NLT paraphrased

He Knows the Plans of My Heart

Many are the plans of my heart, O Lord, but it is Your purpose that prevails. Please direct my steps. How can I possibly understand my own way? All of my ways seem right to me, but, Lord, You weigh my heart. I will seek Your face with all my heart; be gracious to me according to Your promise. I will consider my ways and turn my steps to Your statutes.

PRAYERS, PRAISES, AND PERSONAL NOTES

_____

_____

_____

_____

_____

_____

_____

_____

_____

_____

Prov. 19:21; 20:24; 21:2; Ps. 119:58-59, all paraphrased, A Woman's Walk with God, 61

Apply My Heart to Instruction

Lord, open my eyes that I may see wonderful things in Your law. Teach me Your ways so that I may walk in Your paths. Put Your laws on my mind and write them on my heart. Lord, I will apply my heart to what I observe and learn a lesson from what I see. I will apply my heart to instruction and my ears to words of knowledge.

❦ PRAYERS, PRAISES, AND PERSONAL NOTES ❦

_____

_____

_____

_____

_____

_____

_____

_____

_____

_____

Ps. 119:18; Isa. 2:3b; Heb. 8:10b; Prov. 24:32; 23:12, all paraphrased,
A Woman's Walk with God, 76

Walk in God's Ways

Ever-caring Lord, You love those who love You, and those who seek You find You. You show your love to a thousand generations of those who love You and keep Your commandments. I love You, Lord my God, and will obey all Your requirements, laws, regulations, and commands. I will be careful to obey all the commands You give me; I will show love to You by walking in Your ways and clinging to You. Now, Lord Jesus Christ, prepare me for works of service, so that Your body may be built up.

✾ PRAYERS, PRAISES, AND PERSONAL NOTES ✾

_____

_____

_____

_____

_____

_____

_____

Prov. 8:17; Ex. 20:6; Deut. 11:1, 22 NLT; Eph. 4:12, all paraphrased,
A Woman's Journey Toward Holiness, 117

Soar on Wings Like an Eagle

Everlasting Lord, Creator of the ends of the earth, do I not know? Have I not heard? You do not grow tired or weary. You give strength to the weary and increase the power of the weak. When I grow tired and weary, and stumble and fall, I will hope in You, Lord, for You will renew my strength. Then I will soar on wings like an eagle; I will run and not grow weary; I will walk and not be faint.

PRAYERS, PRAISES, AND PERSONAL NOTES

_____

_____

_____

_____

_____

_____

_____

_____

Isa. 40:28-31 paraphrased, A Woman's Walk with God, *19*

Rest for My Soul

Lord God, my Protector, because I know Your name I will trust in You, for You have never forsaken those who seek You. Teach me the right way to live. Then my soul will find rest in You alone. I will trust in You at all times. I will pour out my heart to You, for You are my refuge. Hear my voice in accordance with Your love. O Lord, renew my life.

🐾 PRAYERS, PRAISES, AND PERSONAL NOTES 🐾

_____

_____

_____

_____

_____

_____

_____

_____

_____

_____

Ps. 9:10; 2 Chron. 6:26b; Ps. 62:1a, 8; 119:149, all paraphrased,
A Woman's Walk with God, 20

Godly Fruit

Lord, fill _____ with the wisdom that comes from heaven, which is first of all pure, then peace-loving, considerate, submissive, full of mercy and good fruit, impartial and sincere. Enable them to live by the fruit of Your Spirit—by love, joy, peace, patience, kindness, goodness, faithfulness, gentleness and self-control. Make them peacemakers who sow in peace in order to raise a harvest of righteousness. Then they will be filled with the fruit of righteousness that comes through You, Jesus Christ, and to Your glory, honor, and praise, O God.

PRAYERS, PRAISES, AND PERSONAL NOTES

_____

_____

_____

_____

_____

_____

James 3:17; Gal. 5:22-23a; James 3:18; Phil. 1:11 all paraphrased

My Refuge and Hiding Place

I will take refuge in You, Lord; let me never be put to shame; deliver me in Your righteousness. For the sake of Your name lead and guide me. Free me from the traps I've set for myself; be my refuge and safe haven. Hide me in the shelter of Your presence. You alone are my refuge and hiding place; protect me from trouble and surround me with songs of deliverance.

PRAYERS, PRAISES, AND PERSONAL NOTES

_____

_____

_____

_____

_____

_____

_____

_____

_____

_____

Ps. 31:1, 3b-4, 20a; 32:7, all paraphrased, A Woman's Walk with God, 23

Rest Securely in Him

Lord, let Your hand rest on me. Then I will not turn away from You; revive me, and I will call on Your name. Restore me, O Lord God Almighty; make Your face shine upon me that I may be saved. As Your beloved child, I will rest secure in You, for You shield me all day long, and because of Your love for me, I will rest between Your shoulders.

🌿 PRAYERS, PRAISES, AND PERSONAL NOTES 🌿

_____

_____

_____

_____

_____

_____

_____

_____

_____

_____

Ps. 80:17a, 18-19; Deut. 33:12, all paraphrased, A Woman's Walk with God, 24

Forgive My Transgressions

Ever-forgiving Savior, my guilt has overwhelmed me like a burden too heavy to bear. By concealing my sins, I do not spiritually prosper. But I will confess my sins and renounce them that I may obtain Your mercy. For who is a God like You, who pardons my sin and forgives my transgressions? You do not stay angry forever but delight to show mercy. Lord, have compassion on me. Tread my sins underfoot and hurl all my iniquities into the depths of the sea.

✥ PRAYERS, PRAISES, AND PERSONAL NOTES ✥

_____

_____

_____

_____

_____

_____

_____

Ps. 38:4; Prov. 28:13; Mic. 7:18-19, all paraphrased, A Woman's Walk with God, *33*

My Hope Comes from the Lord

Ever-living God, by Your strength I will see to it that I do not have a sinful, unbelieving heart that turns away from You. But I will encourage others, and may they encourage me so that we do not become hardened by sin's deceitfulness. Today, Jesus, I will hear Your voice. I will not harden my heart or become rebellious. My soul will find rest in You alone; for my hope comes from You. I will have the faith of God's elect and the knowledge of the truth that leads to godliness—a faith and knowledge resting on the hope of eternal life, which You, who do not lie, promised from the beginning of time.

PRAYERS, PRAISES, AND PERSONAL NOTES

_____

_____

_____

_____

_____

Heb. 3:12-13, 15; Ps. 62:5; Titus 1:1b-2, all paraphrased, A Woman's Walk with God, 25

Devoted to Prayer

Lord, teach me to devote myself to prayer, being watchful and thankful. I kneel before You, Father God, from whom Your whole family in heaven and on earth derives its name. I pray that out of Your glorious riches You may strengthen the people I'm holding up before You with power through Your Spirit in their inner being, so that Christ may dwell in their hearts through faith. And I pray that they may be rooted and established in love.

PRAYERS, PRAISES, AND PERSONAL NOTES

_____

_____

_____

_____

_____

_____

_____

_____

_____

Col. 4:2; Eph. 3:14-17, all paraphrased, A Woman's Walk with God, *34*

Meditate on God's Wonders

O that my soul may be consumed with longing for Your laws at all times, Lord God. Let me understand the teaching of Your precepts; then I will meditate on Your wonders. Strengthen me according to Your Word. Keep me from deceitful ways; be gracious to me through Your law. I have chosen the way of truth; I have set my heart on Your laws. I am holding fast to Your statutes.

PRAYERS, PRAISES, AND PERSONAL NOTES

_____

_____

_____

_____

_____

_____

_____

_____

_____

_____

Ps. 119:20, 27, 28b-31a, all paraphrased, A Woman's Walk with God, 35

Serve Others in Love

Son of Man, You came not to be served, but to serve and to give Your life a ransom for many. Enable me to serve You with all my heart and all my soul. Show me how to serve others in love. Since You have given me freedom, but not the freedom to be selfish and serve myself, I will use my freedom to love and serve others.

PRAYERS, PRAISES, AND PERSONAL NOTES

_____

_____

_____

_____

_____

_____

_____

_____

_____

_____

_____

Matt. 20:28; Josh. 22:5b; Gal. 5:13, all TLB paraphrased,
A Woman's Walk with God, 37

Whole Armor of God

Almighty Lord, I pray that ______________________ may be strong in You and in the power of Your might. May they put on Your whole armor, Lord, that they may be able to stand against the wiles of the devil. For they wrestle not against flesh and blood, but against principalities, against powers, against the rulers of the darkness of this world, against spiritual wickedness in high places. Help them to be sober and vigilant because their adversary the devil, as a roaring lion, walks about, seeking to devour them. Empower them to resist Satan, steadfast in the faith, knowing that the same afflictions are experienced by other Christians around the world.

PRAYERS, PRAISES, AND PERSONAL NOTES

____

____

____

____

____

____

Eph. 6:10-12; 1 Peter 5:8-9, all KJV paraphrased

His Steadfast Love

Lord God, I call to You, and You save me. Evening, morning, and noon I cry out in distress, and You hear my voice. I cast all my cares on You, and You carry them, for You never let the righteous fall. Your steadfast love never ceases; Your mercies never come to an end; they are new every morning; great is Your faithfulness. "The Lord is my portion," says my soul, "therefore I will hope in Him." You are good to me when I wait for You and seek You with all my heart and soul.

🔖 PRAYERS, PRAISES, AND PERSONAL NOTES 🔖

_____

_____

_____

_____

_____

_____

_____

_____

Ps. 55:16-17, 22; Lam. 3:22-25 RSV, all paraphrased, A Woman's Walk with God, 45

Watch in Hope

"Do not be far from me, for trouble is near, and there is no one to help." "But you, O Lord, be not far off; O my strength, come quickly to help me." Rescue me from the hand of my enemy, and enable me to serve You without fear in holiness and righteousness before You all my days. I watch in hope for You, Lord; I wait for You, for You will hear me. I put my hope in You, for I will yet praise You, my Savior and my God.

❧ PRAYERS, PRAISES, AND PERSONAL NOTES ❧

_____

_____

_____

_____

_____

_____

_____

_____

_____

Ps. 22:11, 19 not paraphrased; Luke 1:74-75; Mic. 7:7; Ps. 42:11b paraphrased,
A Woman's Walk with God, 46

Listen to My Prayer

"Listen to my prayer, O God, do not ignore my plea; hear me and answer me." "I said, 'Oh, that I had the wings of a dove! I would fly away and be at rest—I would flee far away and stay in the desert; I would hurry to my place of shelter, far from the tempest and storm.'" "Let the morning bring me word of your unfailing love, for I have put my trust in you. Show me the way I should go, for to you I lift up my soul."

PRAYERS, PRAISES, AND PERSONAL NOTES

_____

_____

_____

_____

_____

_____

_____

_____

_____

Ps. 55:1-2a, 6-8; 143:8, A Woman's Walk with God, 48

Make the Most of Every Opportunity

Lord, my times are in Your hands. When I am with You, I learn wisdom, and from Your mouth come knowledge and understanding. Help me, Holy Counselor, to be wise in the way I act toward others, including outsiders, and to make the most of every opportunity. Teach me how to carry on conversations that are always full of grace and seasoned with salt, so that I may know how to answer everyone.

PRAYERS, PRAISES, AND PERSONAL NOTES

_____

_____

_____

_____

_____

_____

_____

_____

_____

Ps. 31:15a; Prov. 2:6; Col. 4:5-6, all paraphrased, A Woman's Walk with God, 49

Glorify His Name Forever

"I will praise you, O Lord my God, with all my heart; I will glorify your name forever." "Your righteousness reaches to the skies, O God, you who have done great things. Who, O God, is like you?" How great are Your signs, how mighty Your wonders! Your kingdom is an eternal kingdom; Your dominion endures from generation to generation. "I will meditate on all your works and consider all your mighty deeds." Lord, You have done great things for me, and I am filled with joy.

PRAYERS, PRAISES, AND PERSONAL NOTES

_____

_____

_____

_____

_____

_____

_____

_____

Ps. 86:12; Ps. 71:19 not paraphrased; Dan. 4:3 paraphrased; Ps. 77:12 not paraphrased; Ps. 126:3 paraphrased, A Woman's Journey Toward Holiness, 87

God Is My Protection

"The ways of God are without fault. The Lord's words are pure. He is a shield to those who trust him. Who is God? Only the Lord. Who is the Rock? Only our God. God is my protection. He makes my way free from fault. He makes me like a deer that does not stumble; he helps me stand on the steep mountains." "You protect me with your saving shield. You support me with your right hand. You have stooped to make me great. You give me a better way to live, so I live as you want me to." "The Lord lives! May my Rock be praised. Praise the God who saves me!"

☙ PRAYERS, PRAISES, AND PERSONAL NOTES ☙

_____

_____

_____

_____

_____

_____

Ps. 18:30-33, 35-36, 46 NCV

His Counsel Stands Forever

Sovereign Lord, Your counsel stands forever, the purposes and thoughts of Your heart to all generations. "But I cried to him, 'My God, who lives forever. . . . In ages past you laid the foundation of the earth, and the heavens are the work of your hands. Even they will perish, but you remain forever; they will wear out like old clothing. You will change them like a garment, and they will fade away. But you are always the same; your years never end. The children of your people will live in security. Their children's children will thrive in your presence.'" Say, Amen! Blessing, and glory, and wisdom, and thanksgiving, and honor, and power, and might be to You, Almighty God, forever and ever. Amen!

PRAYERS, PRAISES, AND PERSONAL NOTES

_____

_____

_____

_____

Ps. 33:11 KJV paraphrased; Ps. 102:24a–28 NLT not paraphrased; Rev. 7:12 KJV paraphrased

God's Love Continues Forever

"I will always sing about the Lord's love; I will tell of his loyalty from now on. I will say, 'Your love continues forever; your loyalty goes on and on like the sky.' Lord, the heavens praise you for your miracles and for your loyalty in the meeting of your holy ones. Who in heaven is equal to the Lord? None of the angels is like the Lord. When the holy ones meet, it is God they fear. He is more frightening than all who surround him. Lord God All-Powerful, who is like you? Lord, you are powerful and completely trustworthy."

PRAYERS, PRAISES, AND PERSONAL NOTES

_____

_____

_____

_____

_____

_____

_____

Ps. 89:1-2, 5-8 NCV

Loving Our Neighbors

I pray that _____ will grow to love You, Lord our God, with all their hearts, and with all their souls, and with all their strength, and with all their minds. Enable them to love their neighbors as they love themselves. For this is what You, Lord our God, want them to do—to respect You, Lord our God, and do what You tell them to do. You want them to love You, serve You with their whole being, and obey Your commands and laws that You give them for their own good. Prompt them to be careful to obey every command You give them to follow and to love You, Lord our God, to do what You tell them to do and be loyal to You.

🌿 PRAYERS, PRAISES, AND PERSONAL NOTES 🌿

_____

_____

_____

_____

_____

_____

Luke 10:27; Deut. 10:12-13; 11:22, all NCV paraphrased

I Love Your House

"I love your sanctuary, Lord, the place where your glory shines." "Because of your unfailing love, I can enter your house; with deepest awe I will worship at your Temple." "For the word of the Lord holds true, and everything he does is worthy of our trust. He loves whatever is just and good, and his unfailing love fills the earth." "Surely your goodness and unfailing love will pursue me all the days of my life, and I will live in the house of the Lord forever."

🌿 PRAYERS, PRAISES, AND PERSONAL NOTES 🌿

_____

_____

_____

_____

_____

_____

_____

_____

_____

Ps. 26:8; 5:7; 33:4-5; 23:6 NLT

True Love

Ever-loving Lord, help me to love others, for love comes from You. When I am loving, gracious Father, I am born of You, and I know You. When I am unloving, I fail to demonstrate that I know You, Lord, for You are love. This is true love: not that I loved You, God, but that You loved me and sent Your Son as an atoning sacrifice for my sins. Jesus, I love You because You first loved me. But if I say, "I love You, Lord," and yet hate my brothers and sisters, I am a liar. For if I don't love those I see and know, I cannot love You, God, whom I haven't seen. I will follow Your command. I will love You, Lord, and I will love my brothers and sisters.

🌿 PRAYERS, PRAISES, AND PERSONAL NOTES 🌿

_____

_____

_____

_____

_____

_____

1 John 4:7-8, 10, 19-21 paraphrased, A Woman's Walk with God, 32

Love Wisdom

Wise and loving Lord, I pray that _____
will get wisdom and understanding and not forget or
ignore Your words. Help them to hold on to wisdom,
for it will take care of them. May they love it, for it will
keep them safe. Wisdom is the most important thing,
so I pray they will get wisdom. If it costs everything they
have, let them get understanding. Help them to treasure
wisdom, for it will make them great; help them hold on
to it, and it will bring them honor. It will be like flowers in their hair and like beautiful crowns on their
heads.

PRAYERS, PRAISES, AND PERSONAL NOTES

_____

_____

_____

_____

_____

_____

Prov. 4:5-9 NCV paraphrased

What Is Love?

Ever-loving Savior, this is how I know what love is: You laid down Your life for me. And I ought to lay down my life for others. And if I have any of this world's goods, material possessions, and resources for sustaining life and see my fellow believers in need and yet close my heart of compassion against them, how can Your love live and remain in me? As Your dear child, I will not love others merely in theory or in my speech, but in deeds and in truth—in practice and in sincerity. And I will follow this command; I will believe in Your name, Jesus, and I will love others as You commanded me to love them.

✍ PRAYERS, PRAISES, AND PERSONAL NOTES ✍

_____

_____

_____

_____

_____

1 John 3:16-18, 23 AMP paraphrased, A Woman's Walk with God, 82

His Wonderful Love

"I sing to the Lord because he has taken care of me." "Lord, remember your mercy and love that you have shown since long ago." "Your love is wonderful. By your power you save those who trust you." "I trust in your love. My heart is happy because you saved me." I put my trust in You and rejoice; I will forever shout for joy, because You defend me; I love Your name and will be joyful in You.

❧ PRAYERS, PRAISES, AND PERSONAL NOTES ❧

_____

_____

_____

_____

_____

_____

_____

_____

_____

Ps. 13:6; 25:6; 17:7a; 13:5 NCV not paraphrased; Ps. 5:11 KJV paraphrased

Sincere Love

Loving Lord, I won't just pretend that I love others. I will really love them. I will hate what is wrong and stand on the side of the good. I will love others with genuine affection and take delight in honoring them. I will have sincere love for my brothers and sisters in You, Christ, because I was cleansed from my sins when I accepted the truth of the Good News. So I will see to it that I really do love others intensely with all my heart.

PRAYERS, PRAISES, AND PERSONAL NOTES

Rom. 12:9-10; 1 Peter 1:22 NLT, all paraphrased

Love Casts Out Fear

Ever-caring Shepherd, there is no fear in love, but perfect love casts out fear because fear has torment. When I am afraid, I am not made perfect in love. For You have not given me the spirit of fear, but of power, and of love, and of a sound mind. And now what do You, O Lord my God, require of me, but to revere You, to walk in all Your ways, to love You, and to serve You with all my heart and with all my soul.

⚜ PRAYERS, PRAISES, AND PERSONAL NOTES ⚜

_____

_____

_____

_____

_____

_____

_____

_____

_____

1 John 4:18; 2 Tim. 1:7; Deut. 10:12 KJV, all paraphrased

Loving God

O Love eternal, direct my heart into the love of God and into patient waiting for You, Christ. I will keep myself in Your love, looking for Your mercy unto eternal life. Though I have not seen You, Lord Jesus Christ, I love You; though I see You not, yet believing, I rejoice with joy unspeakable and full of glory. Now may Your grace be with all who love You, Lord Jesus Christ, with sincerity of heart. Amen.

PRAYERS, PRAISES, AND PERSONAL NOTES

_____

_____

_____

_____

_____

_____

_____

_____

2 Thess. 3:5; Jude 21; 1 Peter 1:8; Eph. 6:24 KJV, all paraphrased

Love Made Perfect

O God, if I love others, You live in me, and Your love has been brought to full expression through me. I know how much You love me, and I have put my trust in You. God, You are love, and if I live in love, I live in You, and You live in me. And as I live in You, Lord, my love grows more perfect. May my love grow and overflow to others, just as the love of others overflows toward me. I will continue to love others with true Christian love. I will think of ways to encourage others to outbursts of love and good deeds.

❧ PRAYERS, PRAISES, AND PERSONAL NOTES ❧

_____

_____

_____

_____

_____

_____

_____

1 John 4:12b, 16-17a; 1 Thess. 3:12; Heb. 13:1; 10:24 NLT, all paraphrased

Loving God's People

O Lord, enable _____
to give themselves to the service of God's people. Above
all, help them to love others deeply, because love covers
over a multitude of sins. Teach them how to use the gifts
they have received to serve others, faithfully administering Your grace in many different forms. When they
speak, inspire them to speak as one saying the very
words of God. When they serve, empower them to do
it with the strength You provide, so that in all things
You will be praised through Jesus Christ, to Your glory
and power forever and ever. Amen.

🌿 PRAYERS, PRAISES, AND PERSONAL NOTES 🌿

_____

_____

_____

_____

_____

_____

1 Cor. 16:15b NCV; 1 Peter 4:8, 10-11, all paraphrased

Faith Expressed in Love

Lord, I pray that my love for others will overflow more and more. For "if I could speak in any language in heaven or on earth but didn't love others, I would only be making meaningless noise like a loud gong or a clanging cymbal. If I had the gift of prophecy, and if I knew all the mysteries of the future and knew everything about everything, but didn't love others, what good would I be? And if I had the gift of faith so that I could speak to a mountain and make it move, without love I would be no good to anybody. If I gave everything I have to the poor and even sacrificed my body, I could boast about it; but if I didn't love others, I would be of no value whatsoever." Yes, Lord, "what is important is faith expressing itself in love."

⚘ PRAYERS, PRAISES, AND PERSONAL NOTES ⚘

_____

_____

_____

_____

Phil. 1:9a paraphrased; 1 Cor. 13:1-3; Gal. 5:6b not paraphrased, all NLT

Love Will Last Forever

Jesus, I will live a life filled with love for others, following Your example. For You showed by Your life that "love is patient and kind. Love is not jealous or boastful or proud or rude. Love does not demand its own way. Love is not irritable, and it keeps no record of when it has been wronged. It is never glad about injustice but rejoices whenever the truth wins out. Love never gives up, never loses faith, is always hopeful, and endures through every circumstance. Love will last forever." "There are three things that will endure—faith, hope, and love—and the greatest of these is love." Therefore, love will be my highest goal.

✿ PRAYERS, PRAISES, AND PERSONAL NOTES ✿

Eph. 5:2a; 1 Cor. 13:4-8a; 13:13 not paraphrased; 1 Cor. 14:1a paraphrased, all NLT

Where Will Wisdom Be Found?

Who may ascend Your hill, O Lord? Who may stand in Your holy place? Where will wisdom be found? And where is the place of understanding? You understand the way to it, and You know its place. Lord, to fear You is wisdom, and to depart from evil is understanding. Therefore, I will turn my ear to wisdom and apply my heart to understanding. For You have promised to lead me in the way of wisdom and lead me along straight paths.

PRAYERS, PRAISES, AND PERSONAL NOTES

_____

_____

_____

_____

_____

_____

_____

_____

Ps. 24:3; Job 28:12, 23, 28 RSV; Prov. 2:2; 4:11, all paraphrased
A Woman's Walk with God, 47

Listening to the Lord

Lord, from heaven You look down and see all mankind; from Your dwelling place You watch all who live on earth—You form the hearts of all and consider everything I do. Therefore, Lord God, I will listen to what You will say; for You promise peace to me when I do. I will listen to Your instruction and be wise; I will not ignore it. For You will bless me for listening to You, for watching daily at Your doors, for waiting at Your doorway.

🌿 PRAYERS, PRAISES, AND PERSONAL NOTES 🌿

_____

_____

_____

_____

_____

_____

_____

_____

Ps. 33:13-15; 85:8a; Prov. 8:33-34, all paraphrased, A Woman's Walk with God, 50

Gathered in His Name

Jesus, as I join together with others for prayer and sup-
plication, may we be of one accord. For You said that if
two of us shall agree on earth as touching anything that
we shall ask, it shall be done for us by our Father in
heaven. For where two or three of us are gathered
together in Your name, You are there in the midst of us.
O holy Intercessor, answer our prayers because we trust
in You.

PRAYERS, PRAISES, AND PERSONAL NOTES

_____

_____

_____

_____

_____

_____

_____

_____

_____

Acts 1:14a RSV and KJV; Matt. 18:19-20 RSV and KJV;
1 Chron. 5:20b, all paraphrased, A Woman's Walk with God, 62

Teach Me Your Plans

There is no wisdom, no insight, no plan that can succeed against You, Lord. May I always remember that the plans of the righteous are just, but the advice of the wicked is deceitful. Deliver me from the woes of being an obstinate child so that I will not carry out plans that are not yours, forming an alliance, but not by Your Spirit, heaping sin upon sin. If I plot evil, I will go astray. If I plan what is good, I will find love and faithfulness. Deal with me, Your servant, according to Your love and teach me Your decrees, plans, and ways.

❧ PRAYERS, PRAISES, AND PERSONAL NOTES ❧

_____

_____

_____

_____

_____

_____

_____

Prov. 21:30; 12:5; Isa. 30:1; Prov. 14:22; Ps. 119:125, all paraphrased,
A Woman's Walk with God, 63

God Planned the Times

Creator of All, from one man You made every nation of people, that they should inhabit the whole earth, and You planned the times set for them and the exact places where they should live. You did this so we would seek You and reach out for You and find You, though You are not far from us. For it is in You, Sovereign Lord, that we live and move and have our being. Many are the wonders You have done. The things You planned for us—we cannot begin to recount them all to You; were we to speak and tell of them, they would be too many to declare.

PRAYERS, PRAISES, AND PERSONAL NOTES

_____

_____

_____

_____

_____

_____

Acts 17:26-28a; Ps. 40:5, all paraphrased, A Woman's Walk with God, 64

His Plans for Me

"O God, you are my God, earnestly I seek you; my soul thirsts for you, my body longs for you, in a dry and weary land where there is no water." Now I am looking to You and Your strength. I will seek Your face always. I will seek You, Lord, while You may be found; I will call on You while You are near. Your thoughts are precious to me, O God! How vast is the sum of them! Were I to count Your thoughts and plans for me, they would outnumber the grains of sand.

PRAYERS, PRAISES, AND PERSONAL NOTES

_____

_____

_____

_____

_____

_____

_____

Ps. 63:1 not paraphrased; Ps. 105:4; Isa. 55:6; Ps. 139:17-18a paraphrased,
A Woman's Walk with God, 65

Shattered Plans

"My days have passed, my plans are shattered, and so are the desires of my heart." "Do not withhold your mercy from me, O Lord; may your love and your truth always protect me. For troubles without number surround me; my sins have overtaken me and I cannot see." "Be pleased, O Lord, to save me; O Lord, come quickly to help me." For I am still confident of this: I will see Your goodness in the land of the living.

PRAYERS, PRAISES, AND PERSONAL NOTES

_____

_____

_____

_____

_____

_____

_____

_____

_____

Job 17:11; Ps. 40:11-12a, 13 not paraphrased; Ps. 27:13 paraphrased,
A Woman's Walk with God, 66

Be Exalted, O God

O God, my heart is steadfast; I will sing and give praise, even with all my heart. I will praise You, O Lord, among the people, and I will sing praises to You among the nations. For Your mercy is great above the heavens, and Your truth reaches to the clouds. Be exalted, O God, above the heavens and Your glory above all the earth, that Your beloved may be delivered; save me with Your right hand and answer me. God, You have spoken in Your holiness; I will rejoice. I rejoice in You, Lord, yes, and give thanks at the remembrance of Your holiness.

🌸 PRAYERS, PRAISES, AND PERSONAL NOTES 🌸

_____

_____

_____

_____

_____

_____

_____

Ps. 108:1, 3-7a; 97:12, all KJV paraphrased

Teach Me, O Lord

Do good to Your servant, O Lord, and give me encouragement from Your Word; teach me knowledge and good judgment, for I believe in Your commands. Teach me to be temperate, sensible, self-controlled and sound in faith, in love, and in steadfastness and endurance. God of hope, fill me with all joy and peace as I trust in You so that I may overflow with hope by the power of the Holy Spirit.

🍃 PRAYERS, PRAISES, AND PERSONAL NOTES 🍃

_____

_____

_____

_____

_____

_____

_____

_____

_____

Ps. 119:65-66; Titus 2:2 AMP; Rom. 15:13, all paraphrased, A Woman's Walk with God, 78

Assurance of Faith

Lord, I know that faith is the assurance, the confirmation, of the things I hope for, the proof of things I cannot see, and the conviction of their reality. For by the trust born of faith, Your servants of old had divine testimony borne to them by Your written and spoken Word and thus obtained a good report. In the same way strengthen me to fully believe the truth that was written long ago, standing in it steadfastly and firmly, strong in You, Lord, with the certainty of the good news that You died for me, never shifting from trusting You to save me.

🐦 PRAYERS, PRAISES, AND PERSONAL NOTES 🐦

_____

_____

_____

_____

_____

_____

_____

Heb. 11:1-2; Col. 1:23a AMP, all paraphrased, A Woman's Walk with God, 79

Path to Holiness

Holy Spirit, prepare _____
minds for action, to be self-controlled, to set their hopes
fully on the grace that will be given to them when You,
Jesus Christ, are revealed. Urge them to be Your obedient children; deliver them from conforming to the evil
desires they had when they lived in ignorance. For just
as You who called them are holy, so I pray they will be
holy in all they do; "for it is written: 'Be holy, because
I am holy.'"

🌷 PRAYERS, PRAISES, AND PERSONAL NOTES 🌷

_____

_____

_____

_____

_____

_____

_____

_____

1 Peter 1:13-15 paraphrased; 1 Peter 1:16 not paraphrased

Steadfast in Faith

Father God, as Your beloved one, I will be steadfast, immovable, always abounding in Your work, knowing that my labor for You is not in vain. I will continue securely established and steadfast in my faith, without shifting from the hope promised by the Gospel. So then, just as I received You, Christ Jesus my Lord, I will continue to live in You, rooted and built up in You, strengthened in my faith as I was taught, and overflowing with thankfulness.

❧ PRAYERS, PRAISES, AND PERSONAL NOTES ❧

_____

_____

_____

_____

_____

_____

_____

_____

1 Cor. 15:58 NKJV; Col. 1:23a NRSV; Col. 2:6-7, all paraphrased,
A Woman's Pilgrimage of Faith, 226

Sing to the Glory of His Name

"I rejoiced with those who say to me, 'Let us go into the house of the Lord.'" "I praise you, O Lord, with all my heart; I will tell of all your wonders. I will be glad and rejoice in you. I will sing praise to your name, O Most High." I sing to the glory of Your name; I offer You glory and praise. How awesome are Your deeds! Praise be to You, Lord God; let the sound of Your praises be heard.

PRAYERS, PRAISES, AND PERSONAL NOTES

_____

_____

_____

_____

_____

_____

_____

_____

_____

Ps. 122:1; 9:1-2 not paraphrased; Ps. 66:2-3a, 8 paraphrased, A Woman's Walk with God, 93

Hear My Prayer, O Lord

"Hear my prayer, O Lord; listen to my cry for mercy. In the day of my trouble I will call to you, for you will answer me. Among the gods there is none like you, O Lord; no deeds can compare with yours. All the nations you have made will come and worship before you, O Lord; they will bring glory to your name. For you are great and do marvelous deeds; you alone are God."

PRAYERS, PRAISES, AND PERSONAL NOTES

_____

_____

_____

_____

_____

_____

_____

_____

_____

_____

Ps. 86:6-10, A Woman's Walk with God, 94

Our God Is Merciful

"I love the Lord, because he listens to my prayers for help. He paid attention to me, so I will call to him for help as long as I live. The ropes of death bound me, and the fear of the grave took hold of me. I was troubled and sad. Then I called out the name of the Lord. I said, 'Please, Lord, save me!' The Lord is kind and does what is right; our God is merciful. The Lord watches over the foolish; when I was helpless, he saved me. I said to myself, 'Relax, because the Lord takes care of you.' Lord, you saved me from death. You stopped my eyes from crying; you kept me from being defeated. So I will walk with the Lord in the land of the living."

🌿 PRAYERS, PRAISES, AND PERSONAL NOTES 🌿

_____

_____

_____

_____

_____

_____

Ps. 116:1-9 NCV

Growing in Grace

I pray that _____ will be careful and not let evil people lead them away by wrongdoing. May they take care so they will not fall from their strong faith. Let them be rich in everything—in faith, in speaking, in knowledge, in truly wanting to help, and in love. In the same way, may they be strong also in the grace of giving. O God and Jesus our Lord, give them grace and peace more and more, because they truly know You. May they grow in the grace and knowledge of our Lord and Savior Jesus Christ. Glory be to Him now and forever! Amen.

PRAYERS, PRAISES, AND PERSONAL NOTES

_____

_____

_____

_____

_____

_____

_____

2 Peter 3:17; 2 Cor. 8:7; 2 Peter 1:2; 3:18, all NCV paraphrased

His Commands Are a Lamp

Gracious Father, teach me how to bind Your commands and the wisdom of Your words upon my heart and to fasten them around my neck forever. When I walk, they will guide me; when I sleep, they will watch over me; when I awake, they will speak to me. For Your commands are a lamp, and Your teaching is a light, and the corrections of discipline are the way to life.

❧ PRAYERS, PRAISES, AND PERSONAL NOTES ❧

_____

_____

_____

_____

_____

_____

_____

_____

_____

_____

Prov. 6:21-23 paraphrased, A Woman's Walk with God, 95

I Will Seek His Face

Jesus, if it is Your will, it is better that I suffer for doing good than for doing evil. For You died for my sins once for all, the righteous for the unrighteous, to bring me to God. O give me a heart to know You, to know You are Lord. You have never forsaken those who seek You. For You said, "Seek My face." My heart says to You, "I will seek Your face."

PRAYERS, PRAISES, AND PERSONAL NOTES

_____

_____

_____

_____

_____

_____

_____

_____

_____

1 Peter 3:17-18a; Jer. 24:7a; Ps. 9:10b; 27:8 RSV, all paraphrased,
A Woman's Walk with God, 97

Be Generous

Lord, You have commanded me to do good so that I will be rich in good deeds; I will be generous and willing to share. I will serve You and hold fast to You. For those who have served well gain an excellent standing and great assurance in their faith in You, Christ Jesus.

🌺 PRAYERS, PRAISES, AND PERSONAL NOTES 🌺

_____

_____

_____

_____

_____

_____

_____

_____

_____

_____

1 Tim. 6:18; Deut. 13:4b; 1 Tim. 3:13, all paraphrased, A Woman's Walk with God, 98

Perfect Peace

Sovereign God, why is light given to me when I am in misery, and life when I am bitter of soul? Why is life given to me when the way is hidden and You have hedged me in? "What I feared has come upon me; what I dreaded has happened to me. I have no peace, no quietness; I have no rest, but only turmoil." O Holy Comforter, guard me and keep me in perfect and constant peace, for my mind is stayed on You, because I commit myself to You, lean on You, and hope confidently in You.

ᨆ PRAYERS, PRAISES, AND PERSONAL NOTES ᨆ

_____

_____

_____

_____

_____

_____

_____

Job 3:20, 23 paraphrased; Job 3:25-26 not paraphrased; Isa. 26:3 AMP paraphrased,
A Woman's Walk with God, 99

Most Holy Faith

Spirit of God, before I call, You will answer; while I am still speaking, You will hear me. Help me to build myself up in my most holy faith and to pray in Your Spirit. Holy and wise Counselor, teach me all things and remind me of everything that Jesus said. Guide me in Your truth and teach me, for You are God my Savior, and my hope is in You all day long. Humbly I ask that You will guide me in what is right and teach me Your way.

🌺 PRAYERS, PRAISES, AND PERSONAL NOTES 🌺

_____

_____

_____

_____

_____

_____

_____

_____

Isa. 65:24; Jude 20; John 14:26; Ps. 25:5, 9, all paraphrased, A Woman's Walk with God, 108

My Help Comes from the Lord

I will lift up my eyes to the hills. Where does my help come from? My help comes from You, Lord, who made heaven and earth. You will not let my foot be moved; You who keep me will not slumber; indeed, You who keep Israel will neither slumber nor sleep. Lord, You are my keeper; You are my shade at my right hand. The sun will not smite me by day nor the moon by night. You will preserve me from all evil; You will preserve my soul. You will preserve my going out and my coming in from this time forth and forevermore. You are able to save me completely because I come to You, God, through Jesus, who always lives to intercede for me.

❧ PRAYERS, PRAISES, AND PERSONAL NOTES ❧

_____

_____

_____

_____

_____

_____

Ps. 121 KJV and RSV; Heb. 7:25, all paraphrased, A Woman's Walk with God, 109

The Lord's Prayer

Father in heaven, hallowed be Your name. Blessed be Your glorious name, and may it be exalted above all blessing and praise. Your kingdom come; Your will be done on earth as it is in heaven. Teach me to do Your will, for You are my God. Give me this day my daily bread. Teach me, Lord, to treasure the words of Your mouth more than my daily bread. I will forgive others their trespasses, and then You will also forgive my trespasses. And lead me not into temptation, but deliver me from evil. For no temptation has seized me except what is common to others. You are faithful, God; You will not let me be tempted beyond what I am able to bear. But when I am tempted, You will provide a way out so that I can stand up under it. For Yours is the kingdom, and the power, and the glory forever. Amen.

❧ PRAYERS, PRAISES, AND PERSONAL NOTES ❧

_____

_____

_____

*Matt. 6:9b KJV; Neh. 9:5b AMP; Matt. 6:10 KJV; Ps. 143:10a KJV; Matt. 6:11;
Job 23:12b; Matt. 6:12-13a; 1 Cor. 10:13; Matt. 6:13b KJV, all paraphrased,
A Woman's Walk with God, 110*

Hear Me When I Call

"Hear my voice when I call, O Lord; be merciful to me and answer me." "Do not hide your face from me, do not turn your servant away in anger; you have been my helper. Do not reject me or forsake me, O God my Savior." I will seek You, Lord, and You will answer me; deliver me from all my fears. I will wait patiently for You; turn to me and hear my cry. For, God, You have promised that I have this assurance in approaching You: that if I ask anything according to Your will, You hear me. And if I know that You hear me, whatsoever I ask, I know that I have the petitions that I desired of You.

🌺 PRAYERS, PRAISES, AND PERSONAL NOTES 🌺

_____

_____

_____

_____

_____

_____

Ps. 27:7, 9 not paraphrased; Ps. 34:4; 40:1; 1 John 5:14–15 KJV paraphrased,
A Woman's Walk with God, 111

Knowledge of the Truth

Heavenly Father, I approach Your throne of grace with confidence so that I may receive mercy and find grace to help me in my time of need. I lift up before You my requests, prayers, intercessions, and thanksgiving for everyone—for kings, presidents, and all those in authority that we may live peaceful and quiet lives in all godliness and holiness. This is good and pleases You, God my Savior, for You want all people to be saved and to come to the knowledge of the truth. For this reason, I rejoice in You, Lord. I give thanks to You because of Your righteousness, and I sing praises to Your name, O Lord Most High.

≈ PRAYERS, PRAISES, AND PERSONAL NOTES ≈

_____

_____

_____

_____

_____

Heb. 4:16; 1 Tim. 2:1–4; Phil. 3:1; Ps. 7:17, all paraphrased, A Woman's Walk with God, *112*

Lord, Be Exalted!

Lord, I will rejoice in You; I will be joyful in You, God my Savior. I will seek You and rejoice and be glad in You; I love Your salvation and will always say, "Lord, be exalted!" Surely You have granted me eternal blessings and made me glad with the joy of Your presence. "You have made known to me the path of life; you will fill me with joy in your presence, with eternal pleasures at your right hand."

PRAYERS, PRAISES, AND PERSONAL NOTES

_____

_____

_____

_____

_____

_____

_____

_____

Hab. 3:18; Ps. 40:16; 21:6 paraphrased; Ps. 16:11 not paraphrased,
A Woman's Journey Toward Holiness, 198

His Word Stands Forever

Jesus, I'm so grateful that I've been born again, not of perishable seed, but of imperishable seed, through Your living and enduring Word. For I'm like grass, and all my glory is like the flowers of the field; the grass withers and the flowers fall, but, Lord, Your Word stands forever. Heaven and earth will pass away, but Your words will never pass away. "Your statutes are forever right; give me understanding that I may live." "All your words are true; all your righteous laws are eternal." "Your statutes stand firm; holiness adorns your house for endless days, O Lord."

❧ PRAYERS, PRAISES, AND PERSONAL NOTES ❧

_____

_____

_____

_____

_____

_____

1 Peter 1:23-24 [see also Isa. 40:8]; Matt. 24:35 paraphrased;
Ps. 119:144, 160; 93:5 not paraphrased, A Woman's Walk with God, 121

Living Word

O Lord, put Your law in my mind and write it on my heart. For Your word is living and active. Sharper than any double-edged sword, it penetrates even to dividing soul and spirit, joints and marrow; it judges my thoughts and the attitudes of my heart. Nothing in all creation is hidden from Your sight. Everything is uncovered and laid bare before Your eyes; to You I must give account. I will obey Your precepts and Your statutes, for all my ways are known to You.

🌿 PRAYERS, PRAISES, AND PERSONAL NOTES 🌿

_____

_____

_____

_____

_____

_____

_____

_____

Jer. 31:33; Heb. 4:12-13; Ps. 119:168, all paraphrased, A Woman's Walk with God, 122

Keep God's Decrees

May I always keep Your Word with me, to read and study it all the days of my life so that I may learn to revere You, my Lord and my God, and follow carefully all the words of Your law and Your decrees and not consider myself better than other Christians or turn from Your Scripture to the right or to the left. "My heart is set on keeping your decrees to the very end." "I will never forget your precepts, for by them you have renewed my life."

🌿 PRAYERS, PRAISES, AND PERSONAL NOTES 🌿

_____

_____

_____

_____

_____

_____

_____

Deut. 17:19-20a paraphrased; Ps. 119:112, 93 not paraphrased,
A Woman's Walk with God, 124

Share God's Word

"Praise be to you, O Lord; teach me your decrees. With my lips I recount all the laws that come from your mouth. I rejoice in following your statutes as one rejoices in great riches. I meditate on your precepts and consider your ways. I delight in your decrees; I will not neglect your word." By Your grace, I will share Your Word at home, when I walk along the road, when I lie down, and when I get up.

PRAYERS, PRAISES, AND PERSONAL NOTES

_____

_____

_____

_____

_____

_____

_____

_____

_____

Ps. 119:12-16 not paraphrased; Deut. 6:7b paraphrased, A Woman's Walk with God, *125*

Live by God's Spirit

O Holy God, I pray that _____
will live by Your Spirit and not gratify the desires of their
sinful natures. For their sinful natures desire what is
contrary to Your Holy Spirit, and the Spirit what is contrary to their sinful natures. These natures are in conflict with each other, so people do not do what they
want. Rather, I pray they will clothe themselves with
You, Lord Jesus Christ, and not think about how to gratify the desires of their sinful natures.

✥ PRAYERS, PRAISES, AND PERSONAL NOTES ✥

_____

_____

_____

_____

_____

_____

_____

Gal. 5:16-17; Rom. 13:14, all paraphrased

My Rock

Lord Jesus, You alone are my rock and my salvation. You are my fortress; I will never be shaken. I will proclaim Your name. Oh, praise the greatness of my God! You are my rock; Your works are perfect, and all Your ways are just. You are a faithful God who does no wrong; You are upright and just. There is no one holy like You, Lord; there is no one beside You; there is no rock like my God. The Lord lives! Praise be to my rock. Be exalted, O God, the rock, my Savior.

PRAYERS, PRAISES, AND PERSONAL NOTES

_____

_____

_____

_____

_____

_____

_____

_____

Ps. 62:2; Deut. 32:3-4; 1 Sam. 2:2; 2 Sam. 22:47, all paraphrased,
A Woman's Walk with God, 127

Bought with a Price

I know that my body is Your temple—Your very sanctuary—Holy Spirit, who lives within me, whom I have received as a gift from You, Father God. I am not my own; You bought me at a price. Therefore, help me to honor You in my body, mind, and speech. By Your evermerciful grace, I will consecrate myself and be holy because You are the Lord my God. I will keep Your decrees and follow them, for You are the only one who makes me holy.

🌿 PRAYERS, PRAISES, AND PERSONAL NOTES 🌿

_____

_____

_____

_____

_____

_____

_____

1 Cor. 6:19-20 AMP; Lev. 20:7-8, all paraphrased, A Woman's Walk with God, 136

Repentance

May godly sorrow bring me to repentance that leads to deliverance and leaves no regrets, for worldly sorrow brings death. If I conceal my sins, I will not prosper, but I will confess and renounce them and find Your mercy. I will wash my hands, for I am a sinner, and purify my heart, for I am double-minded. I belong to You, Jesus, so I will crucify my sinful nature with its passions and wrong desires. In accordance with Your great love, forgive my sins.

❧ PRAYERS, PRAISES, AND PERSONAL NOTES ❧

_____

_____

_____

_____

_____

_____

_____

_____

2 Cor. 7:10; Prov. 28:13; James 4:8b; Gal. 5:24; Num. 14:19a, all paraphrased,
A Woman's Walk with God, 137

May God's Spirit Rest on Me

O Holy God, I have not received the spirit of the world, but the Spirit who is from You, that I may understand what You have freely given me. Now may Your Spirit rest on me—Your Spirit of wisdom and of understanding, Your Spirit of counsel and of power, Your Spirit of knowledge and of the fear of God.

PRAYERS, PRAISES, AND PERSONAL NOTES

_____

_____

_____

_____

_____

_____

_____

_____

_____

_____

_____

1 Cor. 2:12; Isa. 11:2, all paraphrased, A Woman's Walk with God, 138

Become as Little Children

"Jesus called a small child over to him and put the child among them. Then he said, 'I assure you, unless you turn from your sins and become as little children, you will never get into the Kingdom of Heaven. Therefore, anyone who becomes as humble as this little child is the greatest in the Kingdom of Heaven. And anyone who welcomes a little child like this on my behalf is welcoming me. But if anyone causes one of these little ones who trusts in me to lose faith, it would be better for that person to be thrown into the sea with a large millstone tied around the neck.'" O loving Jesus, I will beware that I do not despise or feel scornful toward or think little of one of these children, for You said that their angels always are in the presence of and look upon the face of Your Father who is in heaven.

🌿 PRAYERS, PRAISES, AND PERSONAL NOTES 🌿

_____

_____

_____

Matt. 18:2-6 NLT not paraphrased; Matt. 18:10 AMP paraphrased

Godly Qualities

Jesus, You have the power of God, by which You have given _____ everything they need to live and to serve You. They have these things because they know You. O Jesus, You called them by Your glory and goodness. Through these You gave them very great and precious promises. With these gifts they can share in being like You, O God. Because they have these blessings, I pray they will do their best to add these things to their lives: to their faith, add goodness; and to their goodness, add knowledge; and to their knowledge, add self-control; and to their self-control, add patience; and to their patience, add service for God; and to their service for God, add kindness for their brothers and sisters in Christ; and to this kindness, add love. If all these things are in them and are growing, they will be useful and productive in their knowledge of You, Lord Jesus Christ.

🌿 PRAYERS, PRAISES, AND PERSONAL NOTES 🌿

_____

_____

2 Peter 1:3-4a, 5-8, all NCV paraphrased

Obey the Lord's Principles

Lord, I pray that_____ will obey
Your principles. Please don't give up on them! How can
they stay pure? By obeying Your Word and following its
rules. I pray they will try their best to find You; don't
let them wander from Your commands. Teach them to
hide Your Word in their hearts that they might not sin
against You. Be good to them so that they will live and
obey Your Word.

❧ PRAYERS, PRAISES, AND PERSONAL NOTES ❧

_____

_____

_____

_____

_____

_____

_____

_____

_____

Ps. 119:8-9b, 10-11, 17, all NLT paraphrased

O Lord, Be Not Far Off

Do not be far from _____,
for trouble is near, and there is no one to help. But You,
O Lord, be not far off. O Lord our strength, come
quickly to help them. Rescue them from the hand of
their enemies and enable them to serve You without fear
in holiness and righteousness before You all their days.
Why are they so downcast? Why are they so disturbed
within themselves? I pray they will put their hope in
You, for they will yet praise You, our Savior and our
God. May they watch in hope for You, Lord, and wait
for You, for You will hear them.

PRAYERS, PRAISES, AND PERSONAL NOTES

_____

_____

_____

_____

_____

_____

Ps. 22:11, 19; Luke 1:74–75; Ps. 42:11; Mic. 7:7, all paraphrased

Pray Without Ceasing

Spirit of God, move upon _____ to pray without ceasing. Quicken them so that they will call upon Your name. Keep them from quenching Your Spirit. Inspire them to pray in Your Spirit on all occasions with all kinds of prayers and requests. With this in mind, prompt them to be alert and always keep on praying for all the saints. Empower them to be devoted to prayer, being watchful and thankful. In everything encourage them to give thanks; for this is Your will, O God, in Christ Jesus.

PRAYERS, PRAISES, AND PERSONAL NOTES

_____

_____

_____

_____

_____

_____

_____

1 Thess. 5:17 KJV; Ps. 80:18b KJV; 1 Thess. 5:19; Eph. 6:18; Col. 4:2; 1 Thess. 5:18, all paraphrased

Man of Sorrows

Jesus, You grew up before Your Father like a tender shoot and like a root out of dry ground. You had no beauty or majesty to attract us to You, nothing in Your appearance that we should desire You. You were despised and rejected by men, a man of sorrows and familiar with suffering. Like one from whom people hide their faces, You were despised, and we esteemed You not. Surely You took up our infirmities and carried our sorrows, and yet we considered You stricken by God, smitten by Him, and afflicted. We all, like sheep, have gone astray; each of us has turned to his own way; and the Lord laid on You, Jesus, the iniquity of us all.

❦ PRAYERS, PRAISES, AND PERSONAL NOTES ❦

_____

_____

_____

_____

_____

_____

Isa. 53:2-6 paraphrased

Is Anything Worth More Than My Soul?

Before Your crucifixion, Jesus, You said to Your disciples that You would suffer many things, be rejected, killed, and after three days rise again. Deliver me from ever denying Your word so that You have to rebuke me as You did Peter, saying, "Get behind me, Satan, for you are not seeing the things of God, but the things of men." Jesus, I will come and listen to You, for if I want to be Your follower, I must put aside my selfish ambition, shoulder my cross, and follow You. If I try to keep my life for myself, I will lose it. But if I give up my life for Your sake and for the sake of the Good News, I will find true life. And how do I benefit if I gain the whole world but lose my own soul in the process? Is anything worth more than my soul?

🔖 PRAYERS, PRAISES, AND PERSONAL NOTES 🔖

_____

_____

_____

_____

Mark 8:31-33 KJV; Mark 8:34–37 NLT, all paraphrased

Watch and Pray

Jesus, just as You said to Peter, are You not also asking me, "Could you not keep watch with Me for one hour?" "'Watch and pray so that you will not fall into temptation. The spirit is willing, but the body is weak.'" Yes, Lord, help me to be careful, or my heart will be weighed down with dissipation, drunkenness, and the anxieties of life, and that day will close on me unexpectedly like a trap. "For it will come upon all those who live on the face of the whole earth." Therefore, I will be always on the watch and will pray that I may be able to escape all that is about to happen and that I may be able to stand before You, Son of Man.

🕮 PRAYERS, PRAISES, AND PERSONAL NOTES 🕮

_____

_____

_____

_____

_____

Matt. 26:40b paraphrased; Matt. 26:41 not paraphrased; Luke 21:34 paraphrased; Luke 21:35 not paraphrased; Luke 21:36 paraphrased

Pierced for My Transgressions

O my Savior, You were pierced for my transgressions; You were crushed for my iniquities; the punishment that brings me peace was laid upon You, and by Your wounds I am healed. You were oppressed and afflicted; yet You did not open Your mouth. You were led like a lamb to the slaughter; as a sheep before her shearers is silent, so You did not open Your mouth. You poured out Your life unto death and were numbered with the transgressors. You bore the sins of many and made intercession for the transgressors. Lord Jesus, You gave Yourself for my sins to rescue me from the present evil age, according to Your will, God and Father, to whom be glory forever and ever. Amen.

PRAYERS, PRAISES, AND PERSONAL NOTES

_____

_____

_____

_____

_____

Isa. 53:5, 7, 12b; Gal. 1:4–5, all paraphrased, A Woman's Walk with God, 184

Everlasting Life

Father God, You showed Your love toward me in that while I was still a sinner, Jesus died on the cross for me. I acknowledge my sin to You and will not hide my iniquity. I confess my transgressions to You, Lord, for You will forgive my guilt and the iniquity of my sin. I confess my sins, believing You are faithful and just to forgive my sins and to cleanse me from all unrighteousness. For, God, You so loved me that You gave Your only Son, Jesus. I believe in You, Jesus, and trust that I will not perish but have everlasting life. I confess with my mouth, Jesus, that You are my Lord and Savior. I believe in my heart that God raised You from the dead, and I am saved. Now I will hold fast to the profession of my faith without wavering, for, Lord, You are faithful to Your promises.

PRAYERS, PRAISES, AND PERSONAL NOTES

_____

_____

_____

_____

Rom. 5:8; Ps. 32:5; 1 John 1:9; John 3:16; Rom. 10:9; Heb. 10:23, all KJV paraphrased

Lead Them to Salvation

Jesus, I pray that godly sorrow will bring _____ to a repentance that leads to salvation and leaves no regret, for worldly sorrow brings death. May Your grace, O God, that has been revealed bring salvation to them. For it is by grace they are saved, through faith—and this not from themselves; it is Your gift, O God—not by our works—so that no one can boast. May they call on Your name, Lord, and be saved. I pray they will confess their sins to You, for You are faithful and just to forgive them and to cleanse them from every wrong. Then they will receive Your blessing, Lord, and have right standing with God their Savior.

PRAYERS, PRAISES, AND PERSONAL NOTES

_____

_____

_____

_____

_____

2 Cor. 7:10; Titus 2:11 NLT; Eph. 2:8-9; Acts 2:21; 1 John 1:9 NLT;
Ps. 24:5 NLT, all paraphrased

Jesus Bore Our Iniquities

O my suffering Savior, by oppression and judgment You were taken away. And who can speak of Your descendants? For You were cut off from the land of the living; for the transgression of Your people You were stricken. You were assigned a grave with the wicked and with the rich in Your death, though You had done no violence, nor was any deceit in Your mouth. Yet it was God's will to crush You and to cause You to suffer, and though the Lord God made Your life a guilt offering, You will see Your offspring and prolong Your days, and Your will, O Lord God, will prosper in Your hand. After the suffering of Your soul, Jesus, You saw the light of life and were satisfied; by Your knowledge, righteous Servant of God, You justified many and bore our iniquities.

❧ PRAYERS, PRAISES, AND PERSONAL NOTES ❧

_____

_____

_____

_____

Isa. 53:8-11 paraphrased

Crucified with Jesus

Jesus, I have been crucified with You, and I no longer live, but You live in me. The life I live in my body, I live by faith in You, Son of God, who loved me and gave Yourself for me. For if I died with You, I will also live with You; if I endure, I will also reign with You. If I suffer for doing right and I endure it, this is well pleasing to You, Lord. For even to this I was called—it is inseparable from my vocation. For You also suffered for me, leaving me Your personal example that I should follow in Your footsteps. Now may I never boast except in Your cross, Lord Jesus Christ, through which the world has been crucified to me and I to the world.

🐾 PRAYERS, PRAISES, AND PERSONAL NOTES 🐾

_____

_____

_____

_____

_____

Gal. 2:20; 2 Tim. 2:11a-12a; 1 Peter 2:20b–21 AMP; Gal. 6:14, all paraphrased,
A Woman's Walk with God, 213

The Nature of a Servant

O Lord, help me to do nothing out of selfish ambition or vain conceit, but in humility to consider others better than myself. For I should look not only to my own interests, but also to the interests of others. My attitude should be the same as Yours, Christ Jesus—who, being in very nature God, did not consider equality with God something to be grasped, but made Yourself nothing, taking the very nature of a servant, being made in human likeness. And being found in appearance as a man, You humbled Yourself and became obedient to death—even death on a cross! Therefore God exalted You to the highest place and gave You the name that is above every name, that at Your name, Jesus, every knee should bow, in heaven and on earth and under the earth, and every tongue should confess that You are Lord, to the glory of God the Father.

PRAYERS, PRAISES, AND PERSONAL NOTES

_____

_____

_____

Phil. 2:3-11 paraphrased

Power of Christ's Resurrection

Whatever was to my profit I now consider loss for Your sake, Christ. What is more, I consider everything a loss compared to the surpassing greatness of knowing You, Christ Jesus my Lord, for whose sake I have lost all things. I consider them rubbish that I may gain You, O Christ, and be found in You, not having a righteousness of my own that comes from the law, but that which is through faith in You—the righteousness that comes from God and is by faith. I want to know You, Christ, and the power of Your resurrection and the fellowship of sharing in Your sufferings, becoming like You in Your death, and so somehow to attain to the resurrection from the dead. For if I am united with You in Your death, I will certainly be united with You in Your resurrection.

🍃 PRAYERS, PRAISES, AND PERSONAL NOTES 🍃

_____

_____

_____

_____

Phil. 3:7-11 KJV; Rom. 6:5, all paraphrased

Jesus Is Life

Jesus, You are the resurrection and the life; I pray that _____ will believe in You and have life, even if they die. For if they live and believe in You, they will never die. Yes, Lord, may they believe that You are the Christ, the Son of God, the one coming to the world. May they have the same hope in You, God—the hope that all people, good and bad, will surely be raised from the dead. "It is the same with the dead who are raised to life. The body that is 'planted' will ruin and decay, but it is raised to a life that cannot be destroyed." Praise be to You, God and Father of our Lord Jesus Christ. In Your great mercy cause them to be born again into a living hope, because Jesus Christ rose from the dead.

🔊 PRAYERS, PRAISES, AND PERSONAL NOTES 🔊

_____

_____

_____

_____

John 11:25-26a, 27; Acts 24:15 paraphrased;
1 Cor. 15:42 not paraphrased; 1 Peter 1:3 paraphrased, all NCV

On God's Right Hand

Yes, Jesus, after You had offered one sacrifice for all my sins for all eternity, You sat down at God's right hand. Now, since I am surrounded by such a huge crowd of witnesses to my life of faith, I will strip off every weight that slows me down, especially the sin that so easily hinders my progress. And I will run with endurance the race that You, O God, have set before me. I will do this by keeping my eyes on You, Jesus, on whom my faith depends from start to finish. For You were willing to die a shameful death on the cross because of the joy You knew would be Yours afterward. Now You are seated in the place of highest honor beside God's throne in heaven.

PRAYERS, PRAISES, AND PERSONAL NOTES

_____

_____

_____

_____

_____

Heb. 10:12 KJV; Heb. 12:1-2 NLT, all paraphrased

Full Redemption

Almighty God, You have rescued me from the dominion of darkness and brought me into the kingdom of the Son You love, in whom I have redemption, the forgiveness of my sins. Yes, God, I am already Your child, and I can't even imagine what I will be like when You return, Jesus Christ my Savior. But I do know that when You come, I will be like You, for I will see You as You really are. I put my hope in You, for with You is unfailing love, and with You is full redemption.

🙚 PRAYERS, PRAISES, AND PERSONAL NOTES 🙚

_____

_____

_____

_____

_____

_____

_____

Col. 1:13-14; 1 John 3:2 NLT; Ps. 130:7, all paraphrased,
A Woman's Pilgrimage of Faith, 200

Worship the Lamb of God

Yes, Jesus, one day I will be among the great multitude that no one can number, of all nations and kindreds and peoples and languages, before the throne and before You. Clothed with white robes and with palms in our hands, we will cry with a loud voice, "Salvation to our God who sits upon the throne and to You, Jesus the Lamb." And all the angels will be standing around the throne and around the elders and the four living creatures. They will fall before the throne on their faces and worship You, O God, saying, "Amen! Blessing and glory, wisdom and thanksgiving, honor and power and might be to our God forever and ever. Amen!"

PRAYERS, PRAISES, AND PERSONAL NOTES

_____

_____

_____

_____

_____

_____

Rev. 7:9-12, all KJV paraphrased

Rock of Protection

Lord, let _____ trust in You; let them never be disgraced. Save them because You do what is right. Listen to them and save them quickly. Be their rock of protection, a strong city to save them. For You are their rock and their protection. For the good of Your name, lead them and guide them. Show Your kindness to them, Your servants. Save them because of Your love. "Those who go to God Most High for safety will be protected by the Almighty." You are their hiding place; O Lord, protect them from troubles and surround them with songs of deliverance. Let them be glad and rejoice in Your love, because You saw their suffering; You knew their troubles.

🐾 PRAYERS, PRAISES, AND PERSONAL NOTES 🐾

_____

_____

_____

_____

Ps. 31:1-3, 16 NCV paraphrased; Ps. 91:1 NCV not paraphrased;
Ps. 32:7 paraphrased; Ps. 31:7 NCV paraphrased

Pure Hearts

Your ways, O holy God, are without fault. Your words are pure. You are a shield to those who trust You. Therefore, I pray _____ will be pure, for to the pure all things are pure, but if they are corrupted and do not believe, nothing is pure. . . . Keep them from the sins of pride; don't let pride rule them. Then they can be pure and innocent of the greatest of sins. May they have clean hands and pure hearts and not lift up their souls to idols or swear by what is false. O God, create pure hearts in them and make their spirits right again. For blessed are they who are pure in their hearts; they will see You, O God.

🐾 PRAYERS, PRAISES, AND PERSONAL NOTES 🐾

_____

_____

_____

_____

_____

Ps. 18:30 NCV; Titus 1:15a; Ps. 19:13 NCV; Ps. 24:4;
Ps. 51:10 NCV; Matt. 5:8, all paraphrased

Great Gain

O Lord, deliver me from all that corrupts my mind, robs me of the truth, and causes me to think that godliness is a means to financial gain. For godliness with contentment is great gain. I brought nothing into the world, and I can take nothing out of it. As Your servant, I will flee from all this and pursue righteousness, godliness, faith, love, endurance, and gentleness. I will fight the good fight of the faith.

PRAYERS, PRAISES, AND PERSONAL NOTES

_____

_____

_____

_____

_____

_____

_____

_____

_____

1 Tim. 6:5b -7, 11-12a paraphrased, A Woman's Walk with God, 139

Be Kind and Loving

May _____ be kind and loving to others, and may they forgive others just as You, O God, forgave them in Christ. They are Your children whom You love, so I pray they will try to be like You. This is how they know what real love is: Jesus, You gave Your life for them. So they should give their lives for their brothers and sisters. I pray _____ will love other people not only with words and talk, but by their actions and true caring. Help them have lives of love just as You, Christ, loved us and gave Yourself for us as a sweet-smelling offering and sacrifice to God.

🌿 PRAYERS, PRAISES, AND PERSONAL NOTES 🌿

_____

_____

_____

_____

_____

_____

_____

Eph. 4:32; 5:1; 1 John 3:16, 18; Eph. 5:2, all NCV paraphrased

Strong in Faith

Jesus, enable _____ to be alert and continue strong in their faith. Help them to have courage and be strong. Empower them to live by what they believe, not by what they can see. May they look closely at themselves and test themselves to see if they are living in the faith. For in You, Christ, they can come before God with freedom and without fear. They can do this through faith in You. O Lord, only one thing concerns me: That they are sure to live in ways that bring honor to the Good News of Christ. And I will hear that they are standing strong with one purpose and working together with other Christians as one for the faith of the Good News.

☙ PRAYERS, PRAISES, AND PERSONAL NOTES ❧

_____

_____

_____

_____

_____

1 Cor. 16:13; 2 Cor. 5:7; 13:5a; Eph. 3:12; Phil. 1:27a, all NCV paraphrased

Hold On to God's Testimonies

Ever-caring Lord, my soul feels dry; quicken me according to Your Word. I declared all my ways to You, and You heard me; now teach me Your statutes. Make me understand the way of Your precepts so I can talk of Your wondrous works. Deliver me from lying as a way of life, and graciously help me to know Your law. For I have chosen the way of truth; I have laid Your judgments before me. I hold on to Your testimonies; Lord, do not put me to shame. Enlarge my heart that I may run in the way of Your commands.

※ PRAYERS, PRAISES, AND PERSONAL NOTES ※

_____

_____

_____

_____

_____

_____

_____

Ps. 119:25-32 KJV paraphrased

Follow Hard After God

O God, You are our God. I pray _____
will search for You and thirst for You like someone in a
dry, empty land where there is no water. Then they will
be content as if they had eaten the best foods. Their lips
will sing, and their mouths will praise You. Cause them
to remember You while they're lying in bed and to think
about You through the night. Quicken them to look to
You, Lord, and to Your strength and to seek Your face
always. May their souls follow hard after You, Lord God,
for Your right hand will uphold them.

PRAYERS, PRAISES, AND PERSONAL NOTES

_____

_____

_____

_____

_____

_____

_____

Ps. 63:1, 5, 6 NCV; 1 Chron. 16:11; Ps. 63:8 KJV, all paraphrased

Understand What Is Right

All-wise Lord, I pray that _____
will understand what is right, just, and fair, and that they
will know how to find the right course of action every
time. May wisdom enter their hearts and knowledge fill
them with joy. Let wise planning watch over them and
understanding keep them safe. May wisdom save them
from evil people, those whose speech is corrupt. Then
wisdom will help them be good and do what is right.

🖋 PRAYERS, PRAISES, AND PERSONAL NOTES 🖋

_____

_____

_____

_____

_____

_____

_____

_____

_____

Prov. 2:9-12 NLT; 2:20 NCV, all paraphrased

Worthy of His Calling

Spirit of God, may I always keep in mind and constantly pray that You may count me worthy of Your calling and that by Your power You may fulfill every good purpose of Yours and every act prompted by faith. I will continue to pray this so that Your name, Lord Jesus, may be glorified in me, and I in You, according to Your grace. For who among the gods is like You, O Lord? Who is like You—majestic in holiness, awesome in glory, working wonders? By Your unfailing love You will lead me, for You have redeemed me. By Your strength You will guide me to Your holy dwelling.

PRAYERS, PRAISES, AND PERSONAL NOTES

_____

_____

_____

_____

_____

_____

_____

2 Thess. 1:11-12; Ex. 15:11, 13, all paraphrased, A Woman's Walk with God, 141

Good Sense

Lord Jesus, I pray that _____ will hold on to wisdom and good sense. May they not let wisdom and good sense out of their sight. For these qualities will give them life and beauty like necklaces around their necks. Then they will go their way in safety, and they will not get hurt. When they lie down, they won't be afraid; when they lie down, they will sleep in peace. They won't be afraid of sudden trouble; they won't fear the ruin that comes to the wicked because, Lord, You will keep them safe. You will keep them from being trapped.

☙ PRAYERS, PRAISES, AND PERSONAL NOTES ☙

_____

_____

_____

_____

_____

_____

_____

Prov. 3:21–26 NCV paraphrased

Help Comes from the Lord

Lord, let _____ lift their eyes unto the hills, from whence comes their help. Their help comes from You, Lord, who made heaven and earth. I pray You will not let their feet be moved. Yes, Lord, You who keep them will not slumber. Behold, You who keep them shall neither slumber nor sleep. For You are their keeper; You are their shade upon their right hand. May the sun not smite them by day nor the moon by night. Lord, preserve them from all evil; preserve their souls. Preserve their going out and their coming in from this time forth and even forevermore

※ PRAYERS, PRAISES, AND PERSONAL NOTES ※

_____

_____

_____

_____

_____

_____

_____

Ps. 121 KJV paraphrased

Delight in God's Commands

Teach _____, O Lord, the way of Your statutes. I pray they will keep Your way to the end. Make them go in the path of Your commands and delight in these. Give them an eagerness for Your decrees; let them not be afflicted with love for money! Turn away their eyes from vanity and quicken them to follow Your ways. Reassure them of Your promises, which are for those who honor You. Help them abandon their shameful ways; may Your laws be all they want in life. May they long to obey Your commandments! O Lord, renew their lives with Your goodness.

PRAYERS, PRAISES, AND PERSONAL NOTES

_____

_____

_____

_____

_____

_____

Ps. 119:33, 35 KJV; Ps. 119:36 NLT; Ps. 119:37 KJV; Ps. 119:38-40 NLT, all paraphrased

Gaze Upon God's Beauty

I love the house where You live, O Lord, the place where Your glory dwells. One thing I ask of You—this is what I seek: that I may dwell in Your house all the days of my life, to gaze upon Your beauty and to seek You in the place where I worship You. "I have seen you in the sanctuary and beheld your power and your glory. Because your love is better than life, my lips will glorify you. I will praise you as long as I live, and in your name I will lift up my hands. My soul will be satisfied as with the richest of foods; with singing lips my mouth will praise you."

🖎 PRAYERS, PRAISES, AND PERSONAL NOTES 🖎

_____

_____

_____

_____

_____

_____

Ps. 26:8; 27:4 paraphrased; Ps. 63:2-5 not paraphrased, A Woman's Walk with God, 67

Every Good Deed

O God, _____ were saved through the sanctifying work of Your Spirit and through belief in the truth. You called them to this through the Gospel that they might share in Your glory, Jesus. So then I pray they will stand firm and hold to the teachings passed on to them. Lord Jesus, may You and God our Father, who love them and by Your grace give them eternal encouragement and good hope, encourage their hearts and strengthen them in every good deed and word.

🔺 PRAYERS, PRAISES, AND PERSONAL NOTES 🔺

_____

_____

_____

_____

_____

_____

_____

2 Thess. 2:13b-17 paraphrased

Serve and Love the Lord

Son of Man, You came not to be served but to serve and to give Your life a ransom for many. I pray that _____ will be very careful to keep Your commandments—to love You, walk in all Your ways, obey Your commands, hold fast to You, and serve You with all their hearts and all their souls. Since they were called to be free, may they not use their freedom to be selfish and indulge their sinful natures; rather, may they serve others in love.

🌿 PRAYERS, PRAISES, AND PERSONAL NOTES 🌿

_____

_____

_____

_____

_____

_____

_____

_____

Matt. 20:28; Josh. 22:5; Gal. 5:13, all paraphrased

An Ever-Present Help in Trouble

Lord, You are my refuge and strength, an ever-present help in trouble. Therefore, I will not fear, though the earth give way and the mountains fall into the heart of the sea, though its waters roar and foam and the mountains quake with their surging. I will be still and know that You are God. For You are with me, Lord Almighty; You are my fortress, God of Jacob. Surely You will be with me always to the very end of the age.

PRAYERS, PRAISES, AND PERSONAL NOTES

_____

_____

_____

_____

_____

_____

_____

_____

Ps. 46:1-3, 10a, 11; Matt. 28:20b, all paraphrased, A Woman's Walk with God, 155

God's Infinite Understanding

Great are You, Lord, and of great power; Your understanding is infinite. Your eyes, O Lord, are in every place, beholding the evil and the good. For Your eyes are upon _____ ways, and You see all their comings and goings. For their ways are before Your eyes, Lord, and You ponder all they do. Instruct them and teach them in the way they should go; guide them with Your eyes. Teach them to do Your will, for You are our God. Your spirit is good; lead them into the land of uprightness.

❧ PRAYERS, PRAISES, AND PERSONAL NOTES ❧

_____

_____

_____

_____

_____

_____

_____

Ps. 147:5; Prov. 15:3; Job 34:21; Prov. 5:21; Ps. 32:8; Ps. 143:10, all KJV paraphrased

He Is Always with Me

O Holy God, You redeemed me in order that the blessing given to Abraham might come to me through You, so that by faith I might receive the promise of the Spirit. Lord God, I know that I live in You, and You live in me, because You have given me Your Spirit. I know that I am Your temple and that Your Spirit lives in me. You are always with me; You hold me by my right hand. You guide me with Your counsel. Now help me to speak, not in words taught to me by human wisdom, but in words taught by You, Holy Spirit, so that I may express spiritual truths in spiritual words.

❦ PRAYERS, PRAISES, AND PERSONAL NOTES ❦

_____

_____

_____

_____

_____

_____

Gal. 3:14; 1 John 4:13; 1 Cor. 3:16; Ps. 73:23-24a; 1 Cor. 2:13, all paraphrased,
A Woman's Walk with God, 151

A Lamp for Their Feet

Lord God, open _____ eyes that they may behold wondrous truths in Your law. Do not hide Your commands from them. Inspire their souls to long for Your laws at all times. Remove reproach and contempt from them so they will keep Your testimonies. May they meditate on Your statutes; let Your testimonies be their delight and counselor. Through Your precepts give them understanding so they will hate every false way. Let Your Word be a lamp for their feet and a light for their path.

🌿 PRAYERS, PRAISES, AND PERSONAL NOTES 🌿

_____

_____

_____

_____

_____

_____

_____

Ps. 119:18-19b, 20, 22, 23b-24; 104:105, all KJV paraphrased

Trumpet Call

Jesus, I am filled with an inexpressible and glorious joy. For I believe You died and rose again, and I am certain that God will bring with You those who have fallen asleep having faith in You. For Lord, You Yourself will come down from heaven with a loud command, with the voice of the archangel and with the trumpet call of God, and the dead who are believers will rise first. After that, if I am still alive and left, I will be caught up together with them in the clouds to meet You, Lord, in the air. And so I will be with You forever.

PRAYERS, PRAISES, AND PERSONAL NOTES

_____

_____

_____

_____

_____

_____

_____

1 Peter 1:8b; 1 Thess. 4:14, 16-17, all paraphrased,
A Woman's Journey Toward Holiness, 88

May They Rest Securely

O our Comforter, give _____
rest from times of trouble. Then they will not turn away
from You; revive them so they will call on Your name.
Restore them, O Lord God Almighty; make Your face
shine upon them that they may be saved. Then they will
find rest in You, Lord, for only You can give them hope.
They will feel safe because there is hope; they will look
around and rest in safety. As Your beloved children, let
them rest securely in You, for You shield them all day
long, and because of Your love for them, may they rest
between Your shoulders.

✿ PRAYERS, PRAISES, AND PERSONAL NOTES ✿

_____

_____

_____

_____

_____

_____

_____

Ps. 94:13a NCV; Ps. 80:18-19; Ps. 62:5 NCV; Job 11:18 NCV; Deut. 33:12b, all paraphrased

Radiant Commands

Lord, Your precepts are right, giving joy to my heart. Your commands are radiant, giving light to my eyes. Your ordinances are sure and altogether righteous. By them I, Your servant, am warned; in keeping them there is great reward. May the words of my mouth and the meditation of my heart be pleasing in Your sight, O Lord, my rock and my redeemer. May I never be lacking in zeal, but help me keep my spiritual fervor, always serving You.

PRAYERS, PRAISES, AND PERSONAL NOTES

_____

_____

_____

_____

_____

_____

_____

_____

Ps. 19:8, 9b, 11, 14; Rom. 12:11, all paraphrased, A Woman's Walk with God, *167*

Full Assurance of Faith

I pray, O God, that _____ will draw near to Your heart, with true hearts in full assurance of faith. Teach them to number their days that they may apply their hearts to wisdom. Yes, Lord, grant them wisdom and understanding; let them not forget or turn away from Your words. I pray they will trust in You with all their hearts and lean not on their own understanding. In all their ways may they acknowledge You and trust You to direct their paths. Let their words and the meditation of their hearts be acceptable in Your sight, O Lord, our strength and redeemer.

🕊 PRAYERS, PRAISES, AND PERSONAL NOTES 🕊

_____

_____

_____

_____

_____

_____

Heb. 10:22a; Ps. 90:12; Prov. 4:5; 3:5-6; Ps. 19:14, all KJV paraphrased

Lord of Lords

"Among the gods there is none like you, O Lord; no deeds can compare with yours." For Lord my God, You are God of gods and Lord of lords; You are the great God, mighty and awesome. You are the Lord my God; I will consecrate myself to You and be holy, because You are holy. I will remember to obey all Your commands and will be consecrated to You. My heart shall rejoice in You because I have trusted in Your holy name.

☙ PRAYERS, PRAISES, AND PERSONAL NOTES ☙

_____

_____

_____

_____

_____

_____

_____

_____

_____

Ps. 86:8 not paraphrased; Deut. 10:17a; Lev. 11:44a; Num. 15:40;
Ps. 33:21 KJV paraphrased, A Woman's Journey Toward Holiness, 20

Live Wisely

The whole body depends on You, Christ, and all the parts of the body are joined and held together. Each part does its own work to make the whole body grow and be strong with love. So I pray _____ will be very careful how they live. Keep them from living like those who are not wise, but help them live wisely. Prompt them to use every chance they have for doing good, because these are evil times. Keep them from being foolish, but may they learn what You want them to do. When they talk, remind them to avoid saying harmful things, but rather help them say what people need—words that will help others become stronger. Then what they say will do good to those who listen to them.

🐦 PRAYERS, PRAISES, AND PERSONAL NOTES 🐦

_____

_____

_____

_____

Eph. 4:16; 5:15-17; 4:29, all NCV paraphrased

God of All Wisdom

God of all wisdom, may I not bring woe on myself by thinking I am wise in my own eyes and clever in my own sight. For if I think I am something when I am nothing, I deceive myself. I will test my own actions. Then I can take pride in myself without comparing myself to someone else. I won't be impressed with my own wisdom. Instead, I'll fear You, Lord, and turn my back on evil. For the greatest among others is Your servant, Lord.

PRAYERS, PRAISES, AND PERSONAL NOTES

_____

_____

_____

_____

_____

_____

_____

_____

_____

Isa. 5:21; Gal. 6:3-4; Prov. 3:7 NLT; Matt. 23:11, all paraphrased,
A Woman's Journey Toward Holiness, 56

God of Our Salvation

O Lord God of our salvation, I have cried day and night before You. I am waiting for the salvation of

_____. Truly my soul waits upon You, God; from You alone comes salvation. I pray that You alone will be their rock and their salvation and their defense. Lead them to Your truth and teach them, for You are the God of our salvation. On You I wait all day. Do not hide Your face far away from them; do not put them away in anger. You are their only hope and help; do not leave them nor forsake them, O God of our salvation.

🙟 PRAYERS, PRAISES, AND PERSONAL NOTES 🙜

_____

_____

_____

_____

_____

_____

_____

Ps. 88:1; Gen. 49:18; Ps. 62:1-2a; 25:5; 27:9, all KJV paraphrased

I Will Trust in Him

"When I am afraid, I will trust in you." Though I am uncertain about what will happen, You, Lord, will go before me and will be with me; You will never leave me nor forsake me. Therefore, I will not be afraid; I will not be discouraged. I will be strong and courageous. I will trust in You at all times; I will pour out my heart to You, for You are my refuge. "I eagerly expect and hope that I will in no way be ashamed, but will have sufficient courage so that now as always Christ will be exalted in my body, whether by life or by death."

✤ PRAYERS, PRAISES, AND PERSONAL NOTES ✤

_____

_____

_____

_____

_____

_____

_____

Ps. 56:3 not paraphrased; Deut. 31:8, 6a; Ps. 62:8 paraphrased;
Phil. 1:20 not paraphrased, A Woman's Journey Toward Holiness, 86

Determine Their Steps

Many are the plans of _____
hearts, O Lord, but it is Your purpose that prevails. In
their hearts they plan their own courses, but I pray You
will determine their steps. May they come to know, O
Lord, that their lives are not their own; it is not for them
to direct their steps. All their ways seem right to them,
but, Lord, You weigh their hearts. I pray they will seek
Your face with all their hearts; be gracious to them
according to Your promises. Deal with them according
to Your love and teach them Your decrees. May they
believe that all Your precepts are right and hate every
wrong path. Your statutes are wonderful; therefore,
may _____ obey them.

PRAYERS, PRAISES, AND PERSONAL NOTES

_____

_____

_____

_____

_____

Prov. 19:21; 16:9; Jer. 10:23; Prov. 21:2; Ps. 119:58, 124, 128–129, all paraphrased

Renewed Day by Day

Merciful Lord, I will not lose heart. Though outwardly I am wasting away, yet inwardly I am being renewed day by day. For I know that my body is Your temple, Holy Spirit, and that You are in me, and that I received You from God. I am not my own; I was bought at a price. Therefore, I will honor You with my body. And by the power that enables You to bring everything under Your control, transform my lowly body so that it will be like Your glorious body.

PRAYERS, PRAISES, AND PERSONAL NOTES

_____

_____

_____

_____

_____

_____

_____

_____

2 Cor. 4:16; 1 Cor. 6:19-20; Phil. 3:21, *all paraphrased,*
A Woman's Journey Toward Holiness, 133

Put On Love

Spirit of holiness, I pray that _____ will put to death whatever belongs to their earthly natures: sexual immorality, impurity, lust, evil desires, and greed, which is idolatry. May they rid themselves of all such things as these: anger, rage, malice, slander, and filthy language from their lips. May they not lie to others, but instead take off their old selves with practices that are wrong and put on new selves, being renewed in knowledge and in Your image, O our Creator. I pray that as God's chosen people, holy and dearly loved, they will clothe themselves with compassion, kindness, humility, gentleness, and patience. May they bear with others, forgiving whatever grievances they may have against others. May they forgive as You, Lord, forgave them. And over all these virtues may they put on love, which binds these all together in perfect unity.

🌿 PRAYERS, PRAISES, AND PERSONAL NOTES 🌿

_____

_____

_____

Col. 3:5, 8-10, 12-14 paraphrased

Fixing My Thoughts on Christ

Jesus, if I conceal my sins, I will not prosper; therefore, I will confess, throw off, and renounce my sins that I may find mercy. "I am deeply sorry for what I have done." Forgive my sin once more, I pray. Since You have gone through suffering and temptation, You are able to help me when I am being tempted. And, as Your dear friend who belongs to You and is bound for heaven, I will fix my thoughts on You, Jesus. I will not throw away my confident trust in You, no matter what happens. I will remember the great reward it brings me! Patient endurance and perseverance are what I need now, so I can continue to do Your will. Then I will receive all that you have promised.

❦ PRAYERS, PRAISES, AND PERSONAL NOTES ❦

_____

_____

_____

_____

Prov. 28:13 KJV paraphrased; Ps. 38:18b NLT not paraphrased; Ex. 10:17a; Heb. 2:18–3:1a NLT; 10:35-36 NLT paraphrased, A Woman's Journey Toward Holiness, 166

Christ's Great Love

I bow in prayer before You, Father, from whom every family in heaven and on earth gets its true name. I ask You, Father, in Your great glory to give _____ the power to be strong inwardly through Your Spirit. I pray, Christ, that You will live in their hearts by faith and that their lives will be strong in love and be built on love. And I pray they and all God's holy people will have the power to understand the greatness of Your love, O Christ—how wide and how long and how high and how deep that love is. Your love is greater than anyone can ever know, but I pray that they will be able to know that love. Then they can be filled with Your fullness, Lord. With Your power working in them, You can do much, much more than anything I can ask or imagine. To You be glory in the church and in Christ Jesus for all time, forever and ever. Amen.

🜚 PRAYERS, PRAISES, AND PERSONAL NOTES 🜚

_____

_____

Eph. 3:14-21 NCV paraphrased

Speak the Truth

Lord, who shall abide in Your sanctuary? Who shall dwell on Your holy hill? I will if I walk uprightly, do what is right, and speak the truth from my heart. If I do not backbite, nor do evil to my neighbor, nor slander others. If in my eyes I condemn a vile person, and honor those that fear You, Lord; and if I honor a promise and do not change it even when it hurts. If I do not charge interest on the money that I lend, nor accept a bribe against the innocent. If I do these things, I shall never be shaken and will stand firm.

PRAYERS, PRAISES, AND PERSONAL NOTES

_____

_____

_____

_____

_____

_____

_____

Ps. 15 KJV paraphrased

Keep Them from Idols

Father God, I ask that _____ will come and listen to You; teach them the fear of You, Lord. I pray that You will keep them from speaking evil and their lips from speaking lies so that they can love life and see many good days. May they keep themselves from idols. Urge them to be careful so that their hearts will not be enticed to turn away and worship other gods and bow down to them. I pray they will submit to You and be at peace with You so that prosperity will come to them. Enable them to receive the law from Your mouth and lay up Your words in their hearts. For then they will delight in You, Almighty One, and will lift up their faces to You, O God.

PRAYERS, PRAISES, AND PERSONAL NOTES

_____

_____

_____

_____

_____

Ps. 34:11-13; 1 John 5:21; Deut. 11:16; Job 22:21-22, 26, all paraphrased

Why, O Lord, Do You Stand Far Off?

"Why, O Lord, do you reject me and hide your face from me?" "For You are the God of my strength; Why do You cast me off? Why do I go mourning because of the oppression of the enemy?" "Why, O Lord, do you stand far off? Why do you hide yourself in times of trouble?" "Even today my complaint is bitter; My hand is listless because of my groaning." "Turn and answer me, O Lord my God! Restore the light to my eyes." "For you are the fountain of life, the light by which we see."

✤ PRAYERS, PRAISES, AND PERSONAL NOTES ✤

_____

_____

_____

_____

_____

_____

_____

_____

Ps. 88:14; Ps. 43:2 NKJV; Ps. 10:1; Job 23:2 NKJV; Ps. 13:3a NLT;
Ps. 36:9 NLT, A Woman's Pilgrimage of Faith, 35

Press On to the Goal

I pray that _____ will train themselves to serve You, Lord. Training their bodies helps them in some ways, but serving You helps them in every way by bringing them blessings in this life and in the future life, too. Free them from caring too much about their own lives. The most important thing is that they complete their mission, the work that You, Lord Jesus, gave them—to tell people the Good News about God's grace. Urge them to press on toward the goal to win the prize for which You have called us heavenward in Christ Jesus. Equip them to fight the good fight of the faith and take hold of the eternal life to which they were called when they made their good confession in the presence of many witnesses.

✿ PRAYERS, PRAISES, AND PERSONAL NOTES ✿

_____

_____

_____

_____

1 Tim. 4:7-8 NCV; Acts 20:24 NCV; Phil. 3:14 NCV; 1 Tim. 6:12, all paraphrased

Restore My Life Again

Merciful Lord, "night pierces my bones; my gnawing pains never rest." "My life is no longer than the width of my hand. An entire lifetime is just a moment to you; human existence is but a breath." Now "I have only a little time left, so leave me alone—that I may have a little moment of comfort." "Though you have made me see troubles, many and bitter . . . restore my life again; from the depths of the earth you will again bring me up." "You shall increase my greatness, and comfort me on every side."

🖋 PRAYERS, PRAISES, AND PERSONAL NOTES 🖋

_____

_____

_____

_____

_____

_____

_____

Job 30:17; Ps. 39:5 NLT; Job 10:20 NLT; Ps. 71:20; Ps. 71:21 NKJV, A Woman's Pilgrimage of Faith, 65

Like Perfumed Oil

Lord, we call to You. Come quickly. Listen to _____ when they call to You. Let their prayers be like incense placed before You, and their praises like the evening sacrifice. Lord, help them control their tongues; help them be careful about what they say. Take away their desire to do evil or to join others in doing wrong. Don't let them be companions of those who do evil. If a good person punished them, that would be kind. If You corrected them, that would be like perfumed oil on their heads.

❧ PRAYERS, PRAISES, AND PERSONAL NOTES ❧

_____

_____

_____

_____

_____

_____

_____

Ps. 141:1-5a NCV paraphrased

Grief and Shame

O Lamb of God, "All day long my disgrace is in front of me. Shame covers my face." "I am worn out from sobbing. Every night tears drench my bed; my pillow is wet from weeping. My vision is blurred by grief; my eyes are worn out because of all my enemies. Go away, all you who do evil, for the Lord has heard my crying." "May they ever be ashamed and dismayed; may they perish in disgrace." "Have compassion on me, Lord, for I am weak. Heal me, Lord, for my body is in agony." "Heal me, O Lord, and I will be healed; save me and I will be saved, for you are the one I praise."

🌿 PRAYERS, PRAISES, AND PERSONAL NOTES 🌿

_____

_____

_____

_____

_____

_____

_____

Ps. 44:15 GOD'S WORD; Ps. 6:6-8 NLT; Ps. 83:17; Ps. 6:2 NLT;
Jer. 17:14, A Woman's Pilgrimage of Faith, 78

Wear God's Armor

Almighty God, I pray that _____
will put on Your full armor so that when the day of evil
comes, they will be able to stand their ground, and after
they have done everything, to stand. Empower them to
stand firm then, with belts of truth buckled around
their waists, with breastplates of righteousness in place,
and with their feet fitted with the readiness that comes
from the Gospel of peace. In addition to all this, enable
them to take up shields of faith, with which they can
extinguish all the flaming arrows of the evil one.
Strengthen them to put on helmets of salvation; equip
them to rightly use the sword of the Spirit, which is Your
Word, O God. Give them grace to be alert and always
to keep on praying for all the saints.

❧ PRAYERS, PRAISES, AND PERSONAL NOTES ❧

_____

_____

_____

_____

Eph. 6:13-17, 18b paraphrased

Redeemed

Merciful Lord, "You have heard my voice: 'Do not hide Your ear from my sighing, from my cry for help.' You drew near on the day I called on You and said, 'Do not fear!' O Lord, You have pleaded the case for my soul; You have redeemed my life. O Lord, You have seen how I am wronged; judge my case." "Stir up Yourself, and awake to my vindication, to my cause, my God and my Lord." "Let those who desire my vindication shout for joy and be glad, and say evermore, 'Great is the Lord, who delights in the welfare of his servant.'"

🌿 PRAYERS, PRAISES, AND PERSONAL NOTES 🌿

_____

_____

_____

_____

_____

_____

_____

Lam. 3:56–59 NKJV; Ps. 35:23 NKJV; Ps. 35:27 NRSV, A Woman's Pilgrimage of Faith, 130

Perfect Love

Ever-loving Lord, I pray that _____
will know the love that You have for them, and may they
trust that love. O God, You are love. May they live in
love and thus live in You, Lord, and You live in them.
This is how love is made perfect in them: that they can
be without fear on the day God judges them, because in
this world they are like You, Lord. Where Your love is,
God, there is no fear, because Your perfect love drives
out fear. It is punishment that makes people fear, so love
is not made perfect in them because of their fears. Yes,
I pray for these dear children that they will live in You
so that when You come back, Christ, they can be without fear and not be ashamed in Your presence.

PRAYERS, PRAISES, AND PERSONAL NOTES

_____

_____

_____

_____

_____

1 John 4:16–18; 2:28, all NCV paraphrased

Enter Not into Temptation

Spirit of God, I'll keep watching and praying that I may not enter into temptation; my spirit is willing, but my flesh is weak. I will take care that this liberty of mine does not somehow become a stumbling block to the weak. For if I sin against members of my family and wound their conscience when it is weak, I sin against You, Christ. To the weak I will become weak so that I might win the weak. I will become all things to all people so that I might by all means save some.

PRAYERS, PRAISES, AND PERSONAL NOTES

_____

_____

_____

_____

_____

_____

_____

_____

Matt. 26:41 NAS95; 1 Cor. 8:9, 12 NRSV;
1 Cor. 9:22 NRSV, all paraphrased, A Woman's Pilgrimage of Faith, 163

Cause Them to Repent

I plead with You, Lord, that _____ will have changes of heart, for they are held captive to sin. I pray they will repent and plead with You to deliver them from being conquered by their sins, saying to You, "We have sinned, we have done wrong, we have acted wickedly." "O Lord, do not your eyes look for truth? You struck them, but they felt no pain; You crushed them, but they refused correction. They made their faces harder than stone and refused to repent." Cause them to turn back to You with all their hearts and souls in the domain of their enemies who took them captive. Cause them to repent and turn to You, O God, so their sins may be wiped out, that times of refreshing may come from You, Lord. Yes, Jesus, there will be more rejoicing in heaven over one sinner who repents than over ninety-nine righteous persons who do not need to repent.

🌿 PRAYERS, PRAISES, AND PERSONAL NOTES 🌿

_____

_____

1 Kings 8:47 paraphrased; Jer. 5:3 not paraphrased;
1 Kings 8:48a; Acts 3:19; Luke 15:7 paraphrased

More Wonderful Than Heaven and Earth

"Praise the Lord! Praise the Lord from the skies. Praise him high above the earth. Praise him, all you angels. Praise him, all you armies of heaven. Praise him, sun and moon. Praise him, all you shining stars. Praise him, highest heavens and you waters above the sky. Let them praise the Lord, because they were created by his command. He put them in place forever and ever; he made a law that will never change. Praise the Lord from the earth, you large sea animals and all the oceans, lightning and hail, snow and mist, and stormy winds that obey him, mountains and all hills, fruit trees and all cedars, wild animals and all cattle, crawling animals and birds, kings of the earth and all nations, princes and all rulers of the earth, young men and women, old people and children. Praise the Lord, because he alone is great. He is more wonderful than heaven and earth."

🌿 PRAYERS, PRAISES, AND PERSONAL NOTES 🌿

_____

_____

Ps. 148:1-13 NCV not paraphrased

Whatever Is True and Admirable

Most holy Lord, whatever is true, whatever is noble, whatever is right, whatever is pure, whatever is lovely, whatever is admirable—if anything is excellent or praiseworthy—I pray that _____ will think about such things. Whatever they have learned or received or heard from those who are godly, or seen in them—I pray they will put it into practice. In the same way, may they let their light shine before others that all may see their good deeds and praise You, Father in heaven. Now may the good work they do be produced by faith, their labor be prompted by love, and their endurance inspired by their hope in You, Lord Jesus Christ.

🌿 PRAYERS, PRAISES, AND PERSONAL NOTES 🌿

_____

_____

_____

_____

_____

Phil. 4:8-9a; Matt. 5:16; 1 Thess. 1:3b, all paraphrased

Turn Mourning into Joy

Now as Your child, I am an heir—heir of God and co-heir with You, Christ, if indeed I share in Your sufferings in order that I may also share in Your glory. I consider that my present sufferings are not worth comparing with the glory that will be revealed in me. And You said, "Comfort, comfort My people." I will rejoice with those who rejoice, and mourn with those who mourn. "I will turn their mourning into joy, I will comfort them, and give them gladness for sorrow."

✦ PRAYERS, PRAISES, AND PERSONAL NOTES ✦

_____

_____

_____

_____

_____

_____

_____

Rom. 8:17-18; Isa. 40:1; Rom. 12:15 paraphrased;
Jer. 31:13b NRSV not paraphrased, A Woman's Pilgrimage of Faith, 213

May Love Abound

All-wise God, may _____ have understanding hearts that seek knowledge. Instill in them the desire to be people of wisdom who hear and increase their learning, and people of understanding who attain wise counsel. Encourage them to trust in You, Lord, and do good; then they will dwell in the land and enjoy safe pasture. And this is my prayer: that their love may abound more and more in knowledge and depth of insight, so that they will be able to discern what is best and be pure and blameless until the day of Christ.

❧ PRAYERS, PRAISES, AND PERSONAL NOTES ❧

_____

_____

_____

_____

_____

_____

_____

Prov. 15:14a KJV; 1:5 KJV; Ps. 37:3; Phil. 1:9-10, all paraphrased

Alpha and Omega

You are the Alpha and the Omega, the beginning and the ending, O God, which is, and which was, and which is to come, the Almighty. Your throne is established of old; You are from everlasting. You remain forever, Your throne from generation to generation. Your name, O Lord, endures forever and your memorial throughout all generations. Therefore, I will praise You with all my heart, and I will glorify Your name forevermore. Now to You, the King eternal, immortal, invisible, the only wise God, be honor and glory forever and ever. Praise be to You, Lord God of Israel, from everlasting to everlasting. Amen and Amen.

PRAYERS, PRAISES, AND PERSONAL NOTES

_____

_____

_____

_____

_____

_____

Rev. 1:8; Ps. 93:2; Lam. 5:19; Ps. 135:13; 86:12; 1 Tim. 1:17; Ps. 41:13, all KJV paraphrased

Hope That Never Disappoints

Since _____ have been made
right with You, God, by their faith, they have peace with
You. This happened through You, Lord Jesus Christ,
who brought them into that blessing of God's grace that
they now enjoy. And I pray they will be happy because
of the hope they have of sharing God's glory. Grant
them Your joy in their troubles, knowing that these
troubles produce patience, and patience produces character, and character produces hope. And this hope will
never disappoint them, because You have poured out
Your love to fill their hearts. You gave them Your love
through the Holy Spirit, whom God has given to them.

PRAYERS, PRAISES, AND PERSONAL NOTES

_____

_____

_____

_____

_____

_____

Rom. 5:1-5 NCV paraphrased

Living Sacrifices

By Your mercies, Lord, I pray that _____ will present their bodies as living sacrifices, holy, acceptable to You, which is their reasonable service. Let them not conformed to this world; but may they be transformed by the renewing of their minds, that they may prove what is that good, and acceptable, and perfect will of Yours, O God. I pray they will not think of themselves more highly than they ought to think, but to think soberly, according as You, Lord, have dealt to them the measure of faith.

PRAYERS, PRAISES, AND PERSONAL NOTES

_____

_____

_____

_____

_____

_____

_____

Rom. 12:1-3b KJV paraphrased

No Need to Fear

When _____ are afraid, I pray they will trust You. For You did not give them a spirit that makes them afraid but a spirit of power and love and self-control. I pray they will not fear, for You are with them. May they not be dismayed, for You are their God. Strengthen them and help them; uphold them with Your righteous right hand. Lord, You are with them; let them not be afraid. What can people do to them? I pray that when they lie down, they will not be afraid; that when they lie down, their sleep will be sweet.

🕊 PRAYERS, PRAISES, AND PERSONAL NOTES 🕊

_____

_____

_____

_____

_____

_____

_____

Ps. 56:3 NCV; 2 Tim. 1:7 NCV; Isa. 41:10; Ps. 118:6; Prov. 3:24, all paraphrased

Fruit of the Spirit

Lord, fill me with the wisdom that comes from heaven, which is first of all pure, then peace-loving, considerate, submissive, full of mercy and good fruit, impartial and sincere. Enable me to live by the fruit of Your Spirit—by love, joy, peace, patience, kindness, goodness, faithfulness, gentleness, and self-control. Make me a peacemaker who sows in peace in order to raise a harvest of righteousness. Then I will be filled with the fruit of righteousness that comes through You, Jesus Christ, and to Your glory, honor, and praise, O God.

✴ PRAYERS, PRAISES, AND PERSONAL NOTES ✴

_____

_____

_____

_____

_____

_____

_____

James 3:17; Gal. 5:22-23a; James 3:18;
Phil. 1:11, all paraphrased, A Woman's Walk with God, 44

Becoming Mature in Christ

Lord Jesus, help _____ to become mature people, growing until they become like You and have Your perfection. Then they will no longer be spiritual babies. Secure them in their faith, Lord, so they will not be tossed about like ships that the waves carry one way and then another. Deliver them from ever being drunk with wine, which will ruin them, but fill them with Your Spirit. Protect them from being influenced by every new teaching they hear from people who will try to fool them. Rather, I pray _____ will grow up in every way into You, Christ, who are the head.

PRAYERS, PRAISES, AND PERSONAL NOTES

_____

_____

_____

_____

_____

_____

_____

Eph. 4:13b–14a; 5:18; 4:14b; 4:15b, all NCV paraphrased

Behold His Glory

Father, the first man is of the earth, earthy: the second man is You, Lord, from heaven. And as I have borne the image of the earthy, I shall also bear Your heavenly image. And may I with open face behold as in a glass Your glory, Lord, and be changed into Your same image from glory to glory; for this comes from You, Holy Spirit. Take this weak mortal body of mine and change it into a glorious body like Your own, using the same mighty power that You will use to conquer everything, everywhere.

🌿 PRAYERS, PRAISES, AND PERSONAL NOTES 🌿

_____

_____

_____

_____

_____

_____

_____

1 Cor. 15:47, 49 KJV; 2 Cor. 3:18 KJV, RSV;
Phil. 3:21 NLT, all paraphrased, A Woman's Journey Toward Holiness, 21

Pursue Godliness

O God, You have called me to be holy. You made me holy by means of Christ Jesus, just as You did all Christians everywhere—whoever calls upon Your name, Jesus Christ, my Lord and theirs. I believe this and will keep myself pure, just as You are pure, Lord. I will love what is good, be self-controlled, upright, holy and disciplined. I will pursue righteousness, godliness, faith, love, endurance, and gentleness.

PRAYERS, PRAISES, AND PERSONAL NOTES

_____

_____

_____

_____

_____

_____

_____

_____

1 Cor. 1:2b NLT; 1 John 3:3 NLT; Titus 1:8;
1 Tim. 6:11b, all paraphrased, A Woman's Journey Toward Holiness, 22

Songs of Thanksgiving

I will sing to You, Lord; O saints of His, give thanks at
the remembrance of His holiness. Surely the righteous
shall give thanks to Your name, O God; the upright
shall dwell in Your presence. We are Your people and
the sheep of Your pasture; we will give thanks to You forever; we will show forth Your praise to all generations.
We come into Your city with songs of thanksgiving and
into Your courtyards with songs of praise. We thank
You and praise Your name.

PRAYERS, PRAISES, AND PERSONAL NOTES

_____

_____

_____

_____

_____

_____

_____

_____

Ps. 30:4 KJV; 140:13 KJV; 79:13 KJV; 100:4 NCV, all paraphrased

Wholly Consecrated

God of grace and mercy, cleanse me from all my impurities and from all my idols. Sanctify me through and through; separate me from profane things; make me pure and wholly consecrated to You. And may my spirit and soul and body be preserved sound and complete and found blameless at Your coming, Lord Jesus Christ. For faithful are You who have called me to Yourself, and utterly trustworthy, and You will also fulfill Your call by hallowing and keeping me.

🕮 PRAYERS, PRAISES, AND PERSONAL NOTES 🕮

_____

_____

_____

_____

_____

_____

_____

_____

Ezek. 36:25b; 1 Thess. 5:23-24 AMP, all paraphrased,
A Woman's Journey Toward Holiness, 24

His Glorious Name

I will stand up and bless You, O Lord my God, forever and ever: blessed be Your glorious name, which is exalted above all blessing and praise. Father God, strengthen and confirm and establish my heart faultlessly pure and unblameable in holiness in Your sight, at the coming of my Lord Jesus Christ, the Messiah, with all His saints, the holy and glorified people of God! Amen, so be it!

🏵 PRAYERS, PRAISES, AND PERSONAL NOTES 🏵

Neh. 9:5b KJV; 1 Thess. 3:13 AMP, all paraphrased,
A Woman's Journey Toward Holiness, 25

Boast in Christ's Cross

O Holy God, deliver me all day and all night long from greedy coveting. Free me from having the soul and life of the wicked who craves and seeks evil and who gives no favor or mercy to others. May I never boast of the cravings of my heart or bless the greedy, for in doing so I would revile You, Lord. May I never boast except in Your cross, Lord Jesus Christ, through which the world has been crucified to me, and I to the world.

❧ PRAYERS, PRAISES, AND PERSONAL NOTES ❧

_____

_____

_____

_____

_____

_____

_____

_____

_____

Prov. 21:26a KJV; Prov. 21:10 AMP; Ps. 10:3;
Gal. 6:14, all paraphrased, A Woman's Journey Toward Holiness, 35

The Light of His Presence

Almighty Ruler of heaven and earth, "You rule the mighty sea and calm the stormy waves." "The skies and the earth belong to you. You made the world and everything in it." "Your arm has great power. Your hand is strong; your right hand is lifted up. Your kingdom is built on what is right and fair. Love and truth are in all you do." O Lord, let me live in the light of Your presence. In Your name I rejoice and continually praise Your goodness. For You are my glorious strength.

🌿 PRAYERS, PRAISES, AND PERSONAL NOTES 🌿

_____

_____

_____

_____

_____

_____

_____

_____

Ps. 89:9, 11, 13-14 not paraphrased; Ps. 89:15b–17a paraphrased; all NCV

Made Right in God's Sight

As in Adam I will die, even so in You, Jesus, I shall be made alive. You were handed over to die because of my sins, and You were raised from the dead to make me right with God. Therefore, since I have been made right in Your sight, O God, I have peace with You because of what You have done for me. Because of my faith, Jesus, You have brought me into this place of highest privilege where I now stand, and I confidently and joyfully look forward to sharing in Your glory. Until that day, may Your grace be poured out on me abundantly, along with faith and love for You, Christ Jesus.

❧ PRAYERS, PRAISES, AND PERSONAL NOTES ❧

_____

_____

_____

_____

_____

_____

1 Cor. 15:22 KJV; Rom. 4:25 NLT; 5:1-2 NLT;
1 Tim. 1:14, all paraphrased, A Woman's Journey Toward Holiness, 37

Freed from All Guilt

Jesus, because I believe in You, I am freed from all guilt and declared right with God—something the Jewish law could not do for me. Therefore, sin shall not be my master, because I am not under law but under grace. What then? Shall I sin because I am not under law but under grace? By no means! I will not set aside Your grace, for if righteousness could be gained through the law, Jesus, You died for nothing!

✿ PRAYERS, PRAISES, AND PERSONAL NOTES ✿

_____

_____

_____

_____

_____

_____

_____

_____

_____

Acts 13:39 NLT; Rom. 6:14-15; Gal. 2:21, all paraphrased,
A Woman's Journey Toward Holiness, 38

Act Justly and Love Mercy

O my Savior, by Your grace, by Your unmerited favor given to me, I will not esteem or think of myself more highly than I ought. I will not have an exaggerated opinion of my own importance, but I will rate my ability with sober judgment, according to the degree of faith You apportioned to me. For You have shown me what is good and what You require of me—to act justly and to love mercy and to walk humbly with You, Lord.

❧ PRAYERS, PRAISES, AND PERSONAL NOTES ❧

_____

_____

_____

_____

_____

_____

_____

_____

Rom. 12:3 AMP; Mic. 6:8, all paraphrased, A Woman's Journey Toward Holiness, 39

Strengthen Me in Every Good Deed

From the beginning, O God, You chose me to be saved through the sanctifying work of Your Spirit and through belief in the truth. You called me to this through the Gospel that I might share in Your glory, Jesus. So then I will stand firm and hold to the teachings that were passed on to me. Lord Jesus Christ, may You and God my Father, who loves me and by Your grace gives me eternal encouragement and good hope, encourage my heart and strengthen me in every good deed and word.

⚘ PRAYERS, PRAISES, AND PERSONAL NOTES ⚘

_____

_____

_____

_____

_____

_____

_____

_____

2 Thess. 2:13b-17 paraphrased, A Woman's Journey Toward Holiness, 40

Foolish Things of the World

O God, Your foolishness is wiser than my wisdom, and Your weakness is stronger than my strength. I will remember what I was when I was called. I was not wise by human standards, nor influential and powerful, nor of high and noble birth. For You chose the foolish things of the world to shame the wise; You chose the weak things of the world to shame the strong. You chose the lowly things of this world and the despised things—and the things that are not—to nullify the things that are, so that I may not boast before You. It is because of You that I am in Christ, who has become for me wisdom from You, O God—that is, my righteousness, holiness, and redemption.

🌿 PRAYERS, PRAISES, AND PERSONAL NOTES 🌿

_____

_____

_____

_____

_____

1 Cor. 1:25-30 paraphrased, A Woman's Journey Toward Holiness, 41

Put On the New Self

Spirit of holiness, strengthen me to kill, deaden, and deprive of power the evil desires lurking in my members, those animal impulses and all that is earthly in me that is sinful: sexual vice, impurity, sensual appetites, unholy desires, and all greed and covetousness, for that is idolatry and the lifting up of self and other created things instead of You, God. I will now rid myself of all these things: anger, rage, malice, slander, and filthy language. I will not lie to others, since I have taken off my old self with its practices and have put on my new self, which is being renewed in knowledge in Your image, O my Creator.

PRAYERS, PRAISES, AND PERSONAL NOTES

_____

_____

_____

_____

_____

Col. 3:5 AMP; Col. 3:8-10, all paraphrased, A Woman's Journey Toward Holiness, 51

Tenderhearted Compassion

Merciful and loving Lord, I will clothe myself, as Your chosen one, who is purified and holy and well beloved by You. I'll put on behavior marked by tenderhearted compassion and mercy, kindness, a lowly opinion of myself, gentle ways, and patience (which is tireless, long-suffering, and has the power to endure whatever comes with good temper). I will be gentle and forbearing with others, and if I have a complaint, difference, or grievance against someone, I will readily pardon that person. Even as You, Lord, freely forgave me, so I must also forgive. And the most important piece of clothing I must wear is love. Love is what binds me with others in perfect harmony.

PRAYERS, PRAISES, AND PERSONAL NOTES

_____

_____

_____

_____

_____

Col. 3:12-13 AMP; Col. 3:14 NLT, all paraphrased, A Woman's Journey Toward Holiness, 52

Armor of Light

Light of the world, I will put aside the deeds of darkness and put on the armor of light. For though my heart was once full of darkness, now I am full of light from You, Lord, and my behavior should show it. For this light within me produces only what is good and right and true. I will try to find out what is pleasing to You. I will take no part in the worthless deeds of evil and darkness; instead, I'll rebuke and expose them. True instruction will be in my mouth, and nothing false will be found on my lips. I will walk with You in peace and uprightness and turn many from sin.

🌿 PRAYERS, PRAISES, AND PERSONAL NOTES 🌿

_____

_____

_____

_____

_____

_____

Rom. 13:12b; Eph. 5:8-11 NLT; Mal. 2:6,
all paraphrased, A Woman's Journey Toward Holiness, 53

Walk in His Spirit

O Holy God, though I was indeed called to freedom, I will not let my freedom be an incentive to my flesh or an excuse for selfishness. I will walk and live habitually in Your Spirit, responsive to and guided by Your Spirit; then I will certainly not gratify the cravings and desires of my flesh. For my sinful nature desires what is contrary to Your Spirit, and Your Spirit desires what is contrary to my sinful nature. They are in conflict with each other, so that I do not do what I want. Rather, I will clothe myself with You, Lord Jesus; I will not think about how to gratify the desires of my sinful nature.

PRAYERS, PRAISES, AND PERSONAL NOTES

_____

_____

_____

_____

_____

_____

Gal. 5:13a, 16 AMP; Gal. 5:17; Rom. 13:14, all paraphrased,
A Woman's Journey Toward Holiness, 54

Healed by Christ's Wounds

Jesus, You said that You rebuke and discipline those whom You love. For You bore my sins in Your body on the tree, so that I might die to sins and live for righteousness; by Your wounds I have been healed. Therefore, Christ, since You suffered in Your body, I will arm myself with the same attitude, because as I suffer in my body, it helps me to be done with sin. For You saved me and called me to live a holy life—not because of anything I have done but because of Your own purpose and grace. By Your divine power, You have given me everything I need for life and godliness through my knowledge of You, Lord, who called me by Your own glory and goodness.

PRAYERS, PRAISES, AND PERSONAL NOTES

_____

_____

_____

_____

Rev. 3:19a; 1 Peter 2:24; 4:1; 2 Tim. 1:9a; 2 Peter 1:3, all paraphrased,
A Woman's Walk with God, 96

Christ's Great Power

God of our Lord Jesus Christ, the glorious Father, I
pray You will give _____ a spirit of
wisdom and revelation so they will know You better. I
pray also that they will have greater understanding in
their hearts so they will know the hope to which You
have called them, and they will know how rich and glorious are Your blessings, God, that You promised Your
holy people. And let them know that Your power is very
great for us who believe. That power is the same as the
great strength You used to raise Christ from the dead
and put Him at Your right side in the heavenly world.

🔖 PRAYERS, PRAISES, AND PERSONAL NOTES 🔖

_____

_____

_____

_____

_____

_____

Eph 1:17-20 NCV paraphrased

Be Loyal

Lord of Righteousness, I pray that I may have a pure heart, for to the pure, all things are pure, but if I am corrupted and do not believe, nothing is pure. In fact, both my mind and my conscience would be corrupted. I will not claim to know You, God, if my actions deny that I know You. For then I would be disobedient and unfit for doing anything good. I will not flatter You with my mouth or lie to You with my tongue; for if I did, my heart would not be loyal to You; nor would I be faithful to Your covenant. I will not swear falsely by Your name and so profane Your name, O God. You are the Lord!

❧ PRAYERS, PRAISES, AND PERSONAL NOTES ❧

_____

_____

_____

_____

_____

_____

Titus 1:15-16; Ps. 78:36-37; Lev. 19:12, all paraphrased,
A Woman's Journey Toward Holiness, 57

Christ Died for Me

Heavenly Father, You demonstrated Your own love to me in this: While I was still a sinner, Christ died for me. For, God, You so greatly loved and dearly prized me that You gave up Your only begotten Son. I believe in, trust in, cling to, and rely on You, Jesus, so that I shall not perish and be lost, but have eternal life. For, God, You did not send Your Son in order to reject and condemn me, but that I might find salvation and be made safe through Jesus my Savior. This is how I know what love is: Jesus Christ, You laid down Your life for me. And I ought to lay down my life for others. I will love others as You have loved me.

PRAYERS, PRAISES, AND PERSONAL NOTES

_____

_____

_____

_____

_____

Rom. 5:8; John 3:16-17 AMP; 1 John 3:16; John 15:12b, all paraphrased,
A Woman's Journey Toward Holiness, 67

Shout to God with Joy

"Clap your hands, all you people. Shout to God with joy. The Lord Most High is wonderful. He is the great King over all the earth! He defeated nations for us and put them under our control. He chose the land we would inherit." "God has risen with a shout of joy; the Lord has risen as the trumpets sounded. Sing praises to God. Sing praises. Sing praises to our King. Sing praises. God is King of all the earth, so sing a song of praise to him. God is King over the nations. God sits on his holy throne. The leaders of the nations meet with the people of the God of Abraham, because the leaders of the earth belong to God. He is supreme."

❧ PRAYERS, PRAISES, AND PERSONAL NOTES ❧

_____

_____

_____

_____

_____

_____

Ps. 47:1-4a, 5-9 NCV

His Good Work in Me

Author and Perfecter of my faith, Your way is perfect; Your Word is flawless. You are my shield, and I will take refuge in You. For who is God besides You, Lord? Who is the rock except You? You arm me with strength and make my way perfect. Therefore, I am convinced that You who began a good work in me will continue developing that good work, perfecting and bringing it to full completion. And I pray, O God, that I may stand perfect and complete in all Your will.

🌿 PRAYERS, PRAISES, AND PERSONAL NOTES 🌿

_____

_____

_____

_____

_____

_____

_____

_____

2 Sam. 22:31-33; Phil. 1:6 AMP; Col. 4:12b KJV, all paraphrased,
A Woman's Journey Toward Holiness, 69

His Plans Stand Firm Forever

Sovereign Lord, the One who never changes, Your plans stand firm forever, the purposes of Your heart through all generations. "In the beginning you laid the foundations of the earth, and the heavens are the work of your hands. They will perish, but you remain; they will all wear out like a garment. Like clothing you will change them, and they will be discarded. But you remain the same, and your years will never end."

🔖 PRAYERS, PRAISES, AND PERSONAL NOTES 🔖

_____

_____

_____

_____

_____

_____

_____

_____

Ps. 33:11 paraphrased; Ps. 102:25-27 not paraphrased,
A Woman's Journey Toward Holiness, 70

Pardon My Iniquity

O merciful Lord, remember Your tender mercies and Your lovingkindnesses, for they have been from everlasting. Remember not the sins of my youth nor my transgressions; according to Your mercy remember me for Your goodness' sake. For Your name's sake, O Lord, pardon my iniquity and my guilt, for they are great. Rebuke me not in Your anger, nor chasten me in Your hot displeasure. Have mercy upon me, for I am weak and faint. My soul is also sorely troubled. Return, O Lord, deliver my soul; oh, save me for Your mercies' sake and Your steadfast love.

PRAYERS, PRAISES, AND PERSONAL NOTES

_____

_____

_____

_____

_____

_____

Ps. 25:6-7, 11 KJV, RSV; 6:1, 2a, 3a, 4 KJV and RSV, all paraphrased,
A Woman's Journey Toward Holiness, 71

God Sees My Every Step

Great are You, Lord, and of great power; Your understanding is inexhaustible and boundless. Your eyes are in every place, keeping watch upon the evil and the good. Your eyes are also on my ways; You see my every step. My ways are directly before Your eyes, and You—who would have me live soberly, chastely, and godly—carefully weigh all my goings. "Teach me to do Your will, for You are my God; let Your good Spirit lead me into a plain country and into the land of uprightness."

PRAYERS, PRAISES, AND PERSONAL NOTES

_____

_____

_____

_____

_____

_____

_____

_____

Ps. 147:5; Prov. 15:3; Job 34:21 ; Prov. 5:21 paraphrased;
Ps. 143:10 not paraphrased, all AMP, A Woman's Journey Toward Holiness, 72

Giving in Secret

Savior of the poor and needy, I will be careful not to do "acts of righteousness" before people, to be seen by them. If I do, I will have no reward from You, Father in heaven. So when I give to the needy, I will not announce it as the hypocrites do in the churches and on the streets, to be honored by people. The truth is, they have received their reward in full. But when I give to the needy, I will not let my left hand know what my right hand is doing, so that my giving may be in secret. Then, Father, You who see what is done in secret will reward me. For, Son of Man, You are going to come in Your Father's glory with Your angels, and then You will reward me according to what I have done.

🌺 PRAYERS, PRAISES, AND PERSONAL NOTES 🌺

_____

_____

_____

_____

_____

Matt. 6:1-4; 16:27 paraphrased, A Woman's Journey Toward Holiness, 73

On Wings of the Dawn

Ever-watchful God, "if I go up to the heavens, you are there; if I make my bed in the depths, you are there. If I rise on the wings of the dawn, if I settle on the far side of the sea, even there your hand will guide me, your right hand will hold me fast." You will lead me when I cannot see, by ways I have not known; along unfamiliar paths You will guide me; You will turn the darkness into light before me and make the rough places smooth. These are the things You will do; You will not forsake me.

PRAYERS, PRAISES, AND PERSONAL NOTES

_____

_____

_____

_____

_____

_____

_____

_____

Ps. 139:8-10 not paraphrased; Isa. 42:16 paraphrased,
A Woman's Journey Toward Holiness, 83

An Understanding Heart

All-wise God, as I go through these difficult changes in
my life, may I have an understanding heart that seeks
knowledge, and not the mouth of a fool that feeds on
foolishness and folly. May I be a person of wisdom who
hears and increases my learning, a person of understanding who attains wise counsel. May I trust in You,
Lord, and do good; then I will dwell in the land and
enjoy safe pasture. And this is my prayer: that my love
may abound more and more in knowledge and depth of
insight, so that I may be able to discern what is best.

PRAYERS, PRAISES, AND PERSONAL NOTES

_____

_____

_____

_____

_____

_____

_____

Prov. 15:14; 1:5 KJV; Ps. 37:3; Phil. 1:9-10a, all paraphrased,
A Woman's Journey Toward Holiness, 84

Giving Thanks

"You are my God, and I will thank you; you are my God, and I will praise your greatness." "Lord, I will thank you with all my heart." "I will thank you, Lord, because you are good." "I will praise God in a song and will honor him by giving thanks." "I will thank the Lord very much; I will praise him in front of many people." "God, I will thank you forever for what you have done. With those who worship you, I will trust you because you are good."

🍂 PRAYERS, PRAISES, AND PERSONAL NOTES 🍂

_____

_____

_____

_____

_____

_____

_____

_____

Ps. 118:28; 138:1a; 54:6b; 69:30; 109:30; 52:9, all NCV

Hiding Place

O our Creator, Your hands made and fashioned _____; give them understanding so that they may learn Your commands. May they know, O Lord, that Your decisions are fair. Let Your unfailing love comfort them, just as You promised. Be their hiding place and shield; may they hope in Your Word. Uphold them according to Your Word, that they may live, and let them not be ashamed of their hope. Hold them up, and they shall be safe, and may they continually have respect for Your statutes. Surround them with Your tender mercies so they may live, and may Your law be their delight.

🌿 PRAYERS, PRAISES, AND PERSONAL NOTES 🌿

_____

_____

_____

_____

_____

Ps. 119:73 KJV; Ps. 119:75a–76 NLT; Ps. 119:114, 116–117 KJV;
Ps. 119:77 NLT, all paraphrased

Future Hope

O God, I will not fret because of evil people nor be envious of the wicked, for the evil person has no future hope. Therefore, I will not let my heart envy sinners, but I will always be zealous for the fear of You. I know also that wisdom is sweet to my soul; if I find it, there is a future hope for me. Yet I do not know the future, and no person can tell me what is to come. I do not have power over the wind to contain it; so I do not have power over the day of my death. Still there is surely a future hope for me, because I know that the One who raised You, Lord Jesus, from the dead will also raise me with You.

🌿 PRAYERS, PRAISES, AND PERSONAL NOTES 🌿

_____

_____

_____

_____

_____

Prov. 24:19-20a; 23:17; 24:14a; Eccl. 8:7-8a; Prov. 23:18a; 2 Cor. 4:14a,
all paraphrased, A Woman's Journey Toward Holiness, *89*

His Everlasting Dominion

Almighty God, be merciful unto us and bless us, and cause Your face to shine upon us that Your way may be known upon the earth and Your saving health among all nations. Let the people praise You, O God; let all the people praise You. O let the nations be glad and sing for joy, for You shall judge the people righteously and govern the nations upon the earth. Let the people praise You, O God; let all the people praise You. Then shall the earth yield her increase; and God, even our own God, shall bless us. Yes, God, You shall bless us, and all the ends of the earth shall fear You.

PRAYERS, PRAISES, AND PERSONAL NOTES

_____

_____

_____

_____

_____

_____

_____

Ps. 67 KJV paraphrased

My Heart Is Broken

Jesus, I will keep awake and watch and pray constantly that I may not enter into temptation; my spirit indeed is willing, but my flesh is weak. "I confess my sins; I am deeply sorry for what I have done." "How long must I struggle with anguish in my soul, with sorrow in my heart every day?" "My grief is beyond healing; my heart is broken." "Have mercy on me, Lord, for I am in distress. My sight is blurred because of my tears. My body and soul are withering away." "I have great sorrow and unceasing anguish in my heart." "I weep with grief; encourage me by your word."

❧ PRAYERS, PRAISES, AND PERSONAL NOTES ❧

_____

_____

_____

_____

_____

_____

Mark 14:38 AMP paraphrased; Ps. 38:18; 13:2a NLT; Jer. 8:18 NLT; Ps. 31:9 NLT; Rom. 9:2; Ps. 119:28 NLT not paraphrased, A Woman's Journey Toward Holiness, 98

Jesus Intercedes for Me

During the days of Your life on earth, Jesus, You offered up prayers and petitions with loud cries and tears to the one who could save You from death, and You were heard because of Your reverent submission. Therefore, You are able to save me completely as I come to You because You always live to intercede for me. And now as I am praying, I will not hold anything against any person; I forgive so that You, Father in heaven, may forgive me of my sins. Into Your hand I commit my spirit and relinquish my life to You, for You have redeemed me.

PRAYERS, PRAISES, AND PERSONAL NOTES

_____

_____

_____

_____

_____

_____

_____

Heb. 5:7; 7:25; Mark 11:25; Ps. 31:5 KJV, all paraphrased,
A Woman's Journey Toward Holiness, 99

His Right Hand

Arise, Lord! Lift up your hand, O God. Do not forget me as I am helpless. You, O God, see my trouble and grief; You consider it to take it in hand. I commit myself to You, for You are my helper. Show the wonder of Your great love to me, You who save me by Your right hand, for I take refuge in You from my foes. Lord, You stand at my right hand when I am needy, to save my life from those who condemn me. You hear my desires when I am afflicted; You encourage me and listen to my cry.

PRAYERS, PRAISES, AND PERSONAL NOTES

_____

_____

_____

_____

_____

_____

_____

_____

Ps. 10:12, 14; 17:7; 109:31; 10:17, all paraphrased,
A Woman's Journey Toward Holiness, 100

The Way Everlasting

Lord, I relinquish _____ into your hands. Search them, O God, and know their hearts; try them and know their thoughts. And see if there be any wicked way in them and lead them in the way everlasting. In the time of Your favor answer them, and in the day of salvation help them and keep them. Say to those who are captives, "Come out," and to those in darkness, "Be free!" O Shepherd of their souls, have compassion on them, guide them, and lead them beside springs of living water.

🕊 PRAYERS, PRAISES, AND PERSONAL NOTES 🕊

_____

_____

_____

_____

_____

_____

_____

_____

Ps. 139:23-24 KJV; Isa. 49:8a, 9a, 10b, all paraphrased

Live by Faith, Not by Sight

Heavenly Father, I am an alien and stranger before You, and a sojourner, as were all my forebears. For here I do not have an enduring city, but I am looking for the city that is to come. Therefore, I live by faith, not by sight. Now faith is being sure of what I hope for and certain of what I do not see. And without faith it is impossible to please You, God, because when I come to You, I must believe that You exist and that You reward me for earnestly seeking You.

🙐 PRAYERS, PRAISES, AND PERSONAL NOTES 🙐

_____

_____

_____

_____

_____

_____

_____

_____

1 Chron. 29:15a KJV; Heb. 13:14; 2 Cor. 5:7; Heb. 11:1, 6, all paraphrased,
A Woman's Journey Toward Holiness, 103

Credited with Righteousness

Father God, "Against all hope, Abraham in hope believed and so became the father of many nations." Yet he did not waver through unbelief regarding Your promise, God, but was strengthened in his faith and gave glory to You, being fully persuaded that You had power to do what You had promised. "This is why 'it was credited to him as righteousness.'" The words "it was credited to him" were written not for him alone, but for me also; You will credit me with righteousness—for I believe in You, who raised Jesus my Lord from the dead.

✤ PRAYERS, PRAISES, AND PERSONAL NOTES ✤

_____

_____

_____

_____

_____

_____

_____

Rom. 4:18a not paraphrased; Rom. 4:20-21 paraphrased; Rom. 4:22 not paraphrased; Rom. 4:23-24 paraphrased, A Woman's Journey Toward Holiness, 104

Here Am I, Send Me

Lord, I hear Your voice saying, "Whom shall I send, and who will go for us?" I say, "Here am I; send me." I delight to do Your will, O my God; yes, Your law is within my heart. Have You not commanded me? Be strong and of a good courage; be not afraid; neither be dismayed: for, O Lord my God, You are with me wherever I go. You will be with me; You will not fail me nor forsake me. Therefore, I will be strong and very courageous that I may observe to do according to all the law; I will turn not from it to the right hand or to the left, that I may prosper wherever I go.

PRAYERS, PRAISES, AND PERSONAL NOTES

_____

_____

_____

_____

_____

_____

Isa. 6:8; Ps. 40:8; Josh. 1:9, 5b, 7a, c, all KJV paraphrased,
A Woman's Journey Toward Holiness, 115

Speak of His Righteousness

O Counselor and Holy Spirit, sent by the Father in Jesus' name, teach me all things. For I am like a deaf person who cannot hear, like a mute who cannot open his mouth; I have become like a person who does not hear, whose mouth can offer no reply. "O Lord, open my lips, and my mouth will declare your praise." Then I will not hide Your righteousness in my heart; I will speak of Your faithfulness and salvation. I will not conceal Your love and Your truth from the great assembly. "My tongue will speak of your righteousness and of your praises all day long."

❧ PRAYERS, PRAISES, AND PERSONAL NOTES ❧

_____

_____

_____

_____

_____

_____

John 14:26a; Ps. 38:13-14 paraphrased; Ps. 51:15 not paraphrased; Ps. 40:10 paraphrased; Ps. 35:28 not paraphrased, A Woman's Journey Toward Holiness, 116

Take His Words to Heart

"When I learned that your laws are fair, I praised you with an honest heart. I will obey your demands, so please don't ever leave me." "With all my heart I try to obey you. Don't let me break your commands. I have taken your words to heart so I would not sin against you." "My lips will tell about all the laws you have spoken. I enjoy living by your rules as people enjoy great riches." "Lord, I call to you with all my heart. Answer me, and I will keep your demands."

⚘ PRAYERS, PRAISES, AND PERSONAL NOTES ⚘

_____

_____

_____

_____

_____

_____

_____

_____

Ps. 119:7-8, 10-11, 13-14, 145 NCV

Serve Wholeheartedly

O Lord my God, I choose to love You and to obey You and commit myself to You, for You are my life. I will serve You wholeheartedly—serving You, Lord, not people. I will care for Your flock entrusted to me. I will watch over it willingly, not grudgingly—not for what I will get out of it, but because I am eager to serve You. I won't lord it over people assigned to my care, but will lead them by my good example. And then, Great Shepherd, when You come, my reward will be a never-ending share in Your glory and honor.

🌿 PRAYERS, PRAISES, AND PERSONAL NOTES 🌿

_____

_____

_____

_____

_____

_____

_____

Deut. 30:20a NLT; Eph. 6:7; 1 Peter 5:2-4 NLT, all paraphrased,
A Woman's Journey Toward Holiness, 118

Seek Good, Not Evil

Lord God Almighty, I will seek good, not evil, that I may live. Then You will be with me. For I know I am loved by You, Lord, that You have chosen me, because the Gospel has come to me not simply with words, but also with power, with the Holy Spirit and with deep conviction. Therefore, I will imitate You, Lord, and those who genuinely love and serve You. In spite of severe suffering, I will welcome the message of the Gospel with the joy given me by the Holy Spirit. As a result, may I become an example to all Christians. And now may Your Word, Lord, ring out from me to people everywhere.

🌿 PRAYERS, PRAISES, AND PERSONAL NOTES 🌿

_____

_____

_____

_____

_____

_____

Amos 5:14a; 1 Thess. 1:4-5a, 6; 1 Thess. 1:7a, 8a NLT, all paraphrased,
A Woman's Journey Toward Holiness, 119

Good News About Christ

Lord Jesus, put Your words in my mouth and cover me with the shadow of Your hand—You who set the heavens in place, who laid the foundations of the earth. You are on my side; I will not fear: what can people do to me? If I suffer as a Christian, I will not be ashamed, but praise You, Lord, that I bear Your name. "For I am not ashamed of this Good News about Christ. It is the power of God at work, saving everyone who believes—Jews first and also Gentiles." "I know very well how foolish the message of the cross sounds to those who are on the road to destruction. But we who are being saved recognize this message as the very power of God."

❧ PRAYERS, PRAISES, AND PERSONAL NOTES ❧

_____

_____

_____

_____

_____

Isa. 51:16a; Ps. 118:6 KJV; 1 Peter 4:16 paraphrased; Rom. 1:16 NLT;
1 Cor. 1:18 NLT not paraphrased, A Woman's Journey Toward Holiness, 120

Obey His Commands

Lord, this is what You told me: "Obey Me, and I will be Your God, and You will be mine. Only do as I say, and all will be well!" I will carefully obey all the commands You give me. I will not add to them nor subtract from them. I will listen to You. For You created me and have cared for me since before I was born. You will be my God throughout my lifetime—until my hair is white with age. You made me, and You will care for me. You will carry me along and rescue me. I will not be afraid, for You are with me.

🔖 PRAYERS, PRAISES, AND PERSONAL NOTES 🔖

_____

_____

_____

_____

_____

_____

_____

Jer. 7:23; Deut. 12:32; Isa. 46:3-4; 43:5a, all NLT paraphrased,
A Woman's Journey Toward Holiness, 121

Obey His Word

Forgiving Savior, streams of tears flow from my eyes, for I have not obeyed Your Word. Before I was afflicted, I went astray, but now I will obey Your Word. I acknowledge my sin to You; I will not cover up my iniquity. I confess my transgressions to You, so that You will forgive the guilt of my sin. For I have been chosen according to Your foreknowledge, Father, through the sanctifying work of Your Spirit, for obedience to You, Jesus Christ, and sprinkling by Your blood. For it is in You that I have redemption through Your blood and the forgiveness of my sins, in accordance with the riches of Your grace, O God.

✦ PRAYERS, PRAISES, AND PERSONAL NOTES ✦

Ps. 119:136, 67; 32:5; 1 Peter 1:2a; Eph. 1:7, all paraphrased,
A Woman's Journey Toward Holiness, 131

Walk in Peace and Uprightness

O God of Truth, deliver me from having a tongue that is a deadly arrow and speaks deceit. May I not speak cordially to my neighbors but in my heart set a trap for them. Deliver me from being false and unfaithful. Help me to return to You truly with all my heart, not just in pretense. Help me to be among the righteous who hate what is false, and not among the wicked who bring shame and disgrace. Then true instruction will be in my mouth, and nothing false will be found on my lips, so that I may walk with You in peace and uprightness and turn many from sin.

🔖 PRAYERS, PRAISES, AND PERSONAL NOTES 🔖

_____

_____

_____

_____

_____

_____

Jer. 9:8; 3:10; Prov. 13:5; Mal. 2:6, all paraphrased,
A Woman's Journey Toward Holiness, 132

His Compassions Never Fail

Lord God, I call to You to deliver _____.
Evening, morning, and noon I cry out in distress for
them, and You hear my voice. I pray they will cast all
their cares on You, for You will sustain them; You never
let righteous people fall. Yes, Lord, because of Your great
love, they are not consumed, for Your compassions
never fail. These are new every morning; great is Your
faithfulness. I pray, Lord, that You will be their portion
as they wait for You. For, Lord, You are good to those
whose hope is in You, to those who seek You.

🌿 PRAYERS, PRAISES, AND PERSONAL NOTES 🌿

_____

_____

_____

_____

_____

_____

_____

_____

Ps. 55:16-17, 22; Lam. 3:22-25, all paraphrased

The Enduring Word of God

"Your word, O Lord, is eternal; it stands firm in the heavens." And I have been born again, not of perishable seed, but of imperishable, through the living and enduring Word of God. Your Word is quick and powerful, sharper than any two-edged sword, piercing even to the dividing asunder of my soul and spirit, and of my joints and marrow, and is a discerner of my thoughts and intents of my heart. Therefore, I will apply my heart to instruction and my ears to words of knowledge. "Give me understanding, and I will keep your law and obey it with all my heart."

PRAYERS, PRAISES, AND PERSONAL NOTES

Ps. 119:89 not paraphrased; 1 Peter 1:23; Heb. 4:12 KJV; Prov. 23:12 paraphrased; Ps. 119:34 not paraphrased, A Woman's Journey Toward Holiness, 134

Apart from Jesus I Can Do Nothing

Jesus, You are the vine; I am the branch. If I remain in You and You in me, I will bear much fruit; apart from You I can do nothing. I did not choose You, but You chose me and appointed me to go and bear fruit—fruit that will last. Then, Father, You will give me whatever I ask in Jesus' name. Lord, this is to Your Father's glory, that I bear much fruit, showing myself to be Your disciple. Therefore, I will be filled with the fruit of righteousness that comes through You, Jesus Christ—to Your glory and praise, O God.

❧ PRAYERS, PRAISES, AND PERSONAL NOTES ❧

_____

_____

_____

_____

_____

_____

_____

John 15:5, 16, 8; Phil. 1:11, all paraphrased, A Woman's Journey Toward Holiness, *135*

May Integrity Protect Me

I know, my God, that You test my heart and are pleased with integrity. Therefore, I will give all things to You willingly and with honest intent. May I be upright so that I may be guided by integrity; may I not be found unfaithful; otherwise, I will be destroyed by my duplicity. For if I am a person of integrity, I will walk securely; but if I take crooked paths, I will be found out. "May integrity and uprightness protect me, because my hope is in you."

PRAYERS, PRAISES, AND PERSONAL NOTES

_____

_____

_____

_____

_____

_____

_____

_____

1 Chron. 29:17a; Prov. 11:3; 10:9 paraphrased; Ps. 25:21 not paraphrased,
A Woman's Journey Toward Holiness, 136

Tell the Nations of His Glory

"Sing to the Lord a new song; sing to the Lord, all the earth. Sing to the Lord and praise his name; every day tell how he saves us. Tell the nations of his glory; tell all peoples the miracles he does, because the Lord is great; he should be praised at all times. He should be honored more than all the gods, because all the gods of the nations are only idols, but the Lord made the heavens. The Lord has glory and majesty; he has power and beauty in his Temple. Praise the Lord, all nations on earth; praise the Lord's glory and power."

🔖 PRAYERS, PRAISES, AND PERSONAL NOTES 🔖

_____

_____

_____

_____

_____

_____

_____

_____

Ps. 96:1-7 NCV

An Undivided Heart

"Teach me your way, O Lord, and I will walk in your truth; give me an undivided heart that I may fear your name." "Show mercy to me according to your great love." "If you are pleased with me, teach me your ways so I may know you and continue to find favor with you." "Guide me with your counsel." "Send forth your light and your truth, let them guide me; let them bring me to your holy mountain, to the place where you dwell."

❧ PRAYERS, PRAISES, AND PERSONAL NOTES ❧

_____

_____

_____

_____

_____

_____

_____

_____

_____

Ps. 86:11; Neh. 13:22; Ex. 33:13a; Ps. 73:24a; 43:3,
A Woman's Journey Toward Holiness, 148

Lead Me on Level Ground

Lord, You are upright; You are my rock. Help me, O God my Savior, for the glory of Your name; deliver me and forgive my sins for Your name's sake. For You sustain the humble but cast the wicked to the ground. "Teach me, and I will be quiet; show me where I have been wrong." "Teach me to do your will, for you are my God; may your good Spirit lead me on level ground." I will praise You, Lord, who counsels me; even at night my heart will instruct me.

🕊 PRAYERS, PRAISES, AND PERSONAL NOTES 🕊

_____

_____

_____

_____

_____

_____

_____

_____

Ps. 92:15a; 79:9; 147:6 paraphrased; Job 6:24; Ps. 143:10 not paraphrased;
Ps. 16:7 paraphrased, A Woman's Journey Toward Holiness, 149

My Life Is Not My Own

Who endowed my heart with wisdom or gave understanding to my mind? Your inspiration, Almighty, gives me understanding. "Your hands made me and formed me; give me understanding to learn your commands." My heart is in Your hand, Lord, as are the water courses; direct and turn my heart whichever way You will. I know, O Lord, that my life is not my own; it is not for me to direct my steps. "Let the morning bring me word of your unfailing love, for I have put my trust in you. Show me the way I should go, for to you I lift up my soul."

PRAYERS, PRAISES, AND PERSONAL NOTES

Job 38:36; Job 32:8b KJV paraphrased; Ps. 119:73 not paraphrased; Prov. 21:1 AMP; Jer. 10:23 paraphrased; Ps. 143:8 not paraphrased, A Woman's Journey Toward Holiness, 150

My Inheritance

"Protect me, God, because I trust in you. I said to the Lord, 'You are my Lord. Every good thing I have comes from you.' As for the godly people in the world, they are the wonderful ones I enjoy." "Those who chase after other gods will be filled with sorrow. I will not take part in their sacrifices or even speak the names of their gods. Lord, you alone are my inheritance, my cup of blessing. You guard all that is mine. The land you have given me is a pleasant land. What a wonderful inheritance!"

✥ PRAYERS, PRAISES, AND PERSONAL NOTES ✥

_____

_____

_____

_____

_____

_____

_____

_____

_____

Ps. 16:1-3 NCV; Ps. 16:4-6 NLT

Teach Me Sound Judgment

To You, O God, belong wisdom and power; counsel and understanding are Yours. Therefore, I will make plans by seeking advice; I will obtain guidance. Otherwise my plans will fail if I lack counsel, but with many advisers they will succeed. Your testimonies also are my delight and my counselors. Lord, teach me sound judgment and knowledge, for I believe in Your commandments. Instruct me and teach me in the way I should go; counsel me and watch over me.

PRAYERS, PRAISES, AND PERSONAL NOTES

_____

_____

_____

_____

_____

_____

_____

Job 12:13; Prov. 20:18; 15:22; Ps. 119:24, 66 KJV; Ps. 32:8, all paraphrased,
A Woman's Journey Toward Holiness, 152

Listen to God's Law

I will hear Your Word, Lord; I will listen to the law of
my God! Your Word will be very near me; it will be in
my mouth and in my heart so I may obey it. "Teach me
what I cannot see; if I have done wrong, I will not do so
again." "I will hasten and not delay to obey your commands." I have declared this day, Lord, that You are my
God, and I will walk in Your ways; I will keep Your
decrees, commands, and laws, and I will obey You.

🔥 PRAYERS, PRAISES, AND PERSONAL NOTES 🔥

_____

_____

_____

_____

_____

_____

_____

_____

_____

*Isa. 1:10; Deut. 30:14 paraphrased; Job 34:32; Ps. 119:60 not paraphrased;
Deut. 26:17 paraphrased, A Woman's Journey Toward Holiness, 153*

Live a Holy Life

O Holy God, I will not be a false witness who speaks lies and sows discord among Christians. I will not be greedy and bring trouble to my family. I will not be perverse and stir up dissension or be a gossip who separates close friends. For it is Your will, Lord, that I should be sanctified, that I should avoid sexual immorality, that I should learn to control my own body in a way that is holy and honorable, and that in this matter I should not wrong others or take advantage of them. Lord, You will punish me for all such sins. For You did not call me to be impure, but to live a holy life.

❧ PRAYERS, PRAISES, AND PERSONAL NOTES ❧

_____

_____

_____

_____

_____

_____

Prov. 6:19 KJV; Prov. 15:27a; 16:28;1 Thess. 4:3-4, 6a-7, all paraphrased,
A Woman's Journey Toward Holiness, 154

He Lives in Me

Lord, I will find out what pleases You. I will obey Your commands, for I live in You, and You live in me. And this is how I know that You live in me: I know it by Your Holy Spirit whom You gave me. So I will make it my goal to please You. Apart from You I can do nothing. O God, deliver me from living the rest of my earthly life for evil human desires, but let me live for Your will. For this world and its desires will pass away, but if I do Your will, I will live forever.

✤ PRAYERS, PRAISES, AND PERSONAL NOTES ✤

_____

_____

_____

_____

_____

_____

_____

_____

Eph. 5:10; 1 John 3:24; 2 Cor. 5:9a; John 15:5b; 1 John 2:17, all paraphrased,
A Woman's Journey Toward Holiness, 165

Firmly Anchored

Lord, I pray that _____ will ponder the direction of their lives and turn to follow Your statutes. Deliver them from evil people who try to drag them into sin; instead, teach them to be firmly anchored to Your law. In the middle of the night, may they get up to thank You because Your laws are right. Encourage them to be friends to everyone who fears You, to anyone who obeys Your orders. O Lord, Your love fills the earth. Teach _____ Your demands. You have done good things for them, as You have promised, Lord. Teach them wisdom and knowledge because they trust Your commands. May Your teachings be worth more to them than thousands of pieces of gold and silver.

🌿 PRAYERS, PRAISES, AND PERSONAL NOTES 🌿

_____

_____

_____

_____

Ps. 119:59, 61 NLT; Ps. 119:62-66, 72 NCV, all paraphrased

Be Holy Because God Is Holy

Merciful and loving God, You disciplined me when I was unruly. Now restore me, and I will return to You, because You are the Lord my God. For I am happy and fortunate to be reproved by You; I will not despise or reject Your correction and discipline. I will not lose heart, become discouraged, utterly spiritless, exhausted, and weary through fear. I will submit to You, Lord, and be at peace with You. I will make level paths for my feet and take only ways that are firm. For You are the Lord my God; I will consecrate myself to You and be holy, because You are holy.

🌾 PRAYERS, PRAISES, AND PERSONAL NOTES 🌾

_____

_____

_____

_____

_____

_____

*Jer. 31:18b; Job 5:17 AMP; 2 Cor. 4:16a AMP; Job 22:21a; Prov. 4:26; Lev. 11:44a,
all paraphrased, A Woman's Journey Toward Holiness, 167*

A Life-Giving Rebuke

God of Wisdom, I will listen to a life-giving rebuke so that I may be at home among the wise. For if I ignore discipline, I despise myself; therefore, I will heed correction and gain understanding. I will get the truth and will never sell it; I will also get wisdom, discipline, and discernment. I will listen to counsel, receive instruction, and accept correction that I may be wise. O Lord, "give me understanding and I will obey your law; I will put it into practice with all my heart."

🌿 PRAYERS, PRAISES, AND PERSONAL NOTES 🌿

_____

_____

_____

_____

_____

_____

_____

_____

Prov. 15:31-32; Prov. 23:23 NLT; Prov. 19:20a AMP paraphrased;
Ps. 119:34 NLT not paraphrased, A Woman's Journey Toward Holiness, 168

Keep Spiritually Fit

Master Coach, I will train myself toward godliness and keep myself spiritually fit. For physical training is of some value to me, but godliness and spiritual training are useful and of value in everything, for they hold promise for my present life and also for my life to come. I will consider my life worth nothing to me, if only I may finish the race and complete the task You have given me, Lord Jesus—the task of telling others the Good News of God's grace. I will press on toward the goal to win the prize for which You, Lord, have called me heavenward in Christ Jesus.

PRAYERS, PRAISES, AND PERSONAL NOTES

_____

_____

_____

_____

_____

_____

1 Tim. 4:7b-8 AMP; Acts 20:24; Phil. 3:14, all paraphrased,
A Woman's Journey Toward Holiness, 169

Fight the Good Fight of Faith

Almighty God, I will fight the good fight of faith. I will take hold of the eternal life to which I was called when I made my good confession of faith in the presence of many witnesses. I will let endurance, steadfastness, patience, and perseverance have full play and do a thorough work in my life, so that I may be mature and complete, lacking in nothing. I will keep hold of the deep truths of the faith with a clear conscience. Jesus, You are coming soon. Therefore, I will hold on to what I have so that no one will take my crown. And when You appear, I will receive the crown of glory that will never fade away.

🕊 PRAYERS, PRAISES, AND PERSONAL NOTES 🕊

_____

_____

_____

_____

_____

1 Tim. 6:12; James 1:4 AMP, NIV; 1 Tim. 3:9; Rev. 3:11; 1 Peter 5:4, all paraphrased,
A Woman's Journey Toward Holiness, 170

His Teaching Is a Light

"Answer me when I pray to you, my God who does what is right. Make things easier for me when I am in trouble. Have mercy on me and hear my prayer." O Lord, You love justice and will not leave me, for I worship You. You will always protect me. Teach me how short my life really is so that I may be wise. "My God, I want to do what you want. Your teachings are in my heart." So I will trust You, God, and will not forget what You have done. I will obey Your commands. These commands are like a lamp; this teaching is like a light. And the correction that comes from it will help me have life.

🔖 PRAYERS, PRAISES, AND PERSONAL NOTES 🔖

_____

_____

_____

_____

_____

_____

Ps. 4:1 not paraphrased; Ps. 37:28; 90:12 paraphrased; 40:8 not paraphrased;
Ps. 78:7; Prov. 6:23 paraphrased, all NCV

He Rescues the Poor

"My whole being will exclaim, 'Who is like you, O Lord? You rescue the poor from those too strong for them, the poor and needy from those who rob them.'" You uphold the cause of the oppressed and give food to the hungry. You, Lord, set prisoners free. Therefore, I will not exploit the poor, because they are poor and will not crush the needy in court. Yes, I will speak up for the poor and helpless and see that they get justice.

PRAYERS, PRAISES, AND PERSONAL NOTES

_____

_____

_____

_____

_____

_____

_____

_____

Ps. 35:10 not paraphrased; Ps. 146:7; Prov. 22:22; Prov. 31:9 NLT paraphrased,
A Woman's Journey Toward Holiness, 181

Reach Out to the Poor

Lord, I have freely received; therefore, I will freely give.
I will open my hands to the poor; yes, I will reach out
to the needy with my hands filled. Then I will know the
blessing of generously sharing my food with the poor.
By being generous, my soul will prosper and be
enriched; when I refresh others, I will myself be
refreshed.

❧ PRAYERS, PRAISES, AND PERSONAL NOTES ❧

_____

_____

_____

_____

_____

_____

_____

_____

_____

_____

Matt. 10:8b; Prov. 31:20 AMP; Prov. 22:9; 11:25, all paraphrased,
A Woman's Journey Toward Holiness, 180

Loose the Chains of Injustice

Lord, the kind of fast You have chosen is not just a day for me to humble myself. The kind of fasting You have chosen for me is to loose the chains of injustice and untie the cords of the yoke, to set the oppressed free and break every yoke. It is to share my food with the hungry and to provide the poor wanderer with shelter—when I see the naked, to clothe them, and not to turn away from my own flesh and blood. And if I spend myself in behalf of the hungry and satisfy the needs of the oppressed, then my light will rise in the darkness, and my night will become like the noonday.

❧ PRAYERS, PRAISES, AND PERSONAL NOTES ❧

_____

_____

_____

_____

_____

_____

_____

Isa. 58:5a, 6-7, 10 paraphrased, A Woman's Journey Toward Holiness, 182

Give Generously

O generous and ever-giving God, a little that a righteous person has is better than the riches of the wicked. Therefore, I will be among the righteous who show mercy and give generously. Out of the most severe trial, I will overflow with joy, and in extreme poverty I will well up in rich generosity. I will give as much as I am able, and even beyond my ability. I will give, and it shall be given to me—good measure, pressed down, and shaken together, and running over, shall others give to me. For with the same measure that I use when I give to others shall it be measured to me again.

PRAYERS, PRAISES, AND PERSONAL NOTES

_____

_____

_____

_____

_____

_____

Ps. 37:16, 21b KJV; 2 Cor. 8:2-3; Luke 6:38 KJV, all paraphrased,
A Woman's Journey Toward Holiness, 183

Practice Hospitality to Strangers

Ever kind and giving Lord, teach me how to use whatever gift I have received to serve others, faithfully administering Your grace in its various forms. Then I will do good deeds, as one who has brought up children, who has practiced hospitality to strangers, who has washed the feet of the saints, who has helped to relieve the distressed, and devoted myself to doing good in every way. I will also consider how I may spur others on toward love and good deeds. I will let my light so shine before others that they may see my good works and glorify You, Father, who are in heaven.

❧ PRAYERS, PRAISES, AND PERSONAL NOTES ❧

_____

_____

_____

_____

_____

_____

1 Peter 4:10; 1 Tim. 5:10 AMP; Heb. 10:24; Matt. 5:16 KJV, all paraphrased,
A Woman's Journey Toward Holiness, 184

Be Rich in Good Deeds

Lord, I will honor You with my income and with the first fruits of all my labor. For You commanded me to do good, to be rich in good deeds, and to be generous and willing to share. By Your grace and my own hard work, I will help the weak, remembering Your very words, Lord Jesus: "It is more blessed to give than to receive." Strengthen me so that I will not grow weary in doing good, for at the proper time I will reap a harvest if I do not give up. Therefore, as I have opportunity, I will do good to all people, especially to those who belong to the family of believers.

_____

_____

_____

_____

_____

_____

Prov. 3:9; 1 Tim. 6:18 paraphrased; Acts 20:35b not paraphrased; Gal. 6:9-10 paraphrased, A Woman's Journey Toward Holiness, 185

Contribute to the Needs of Others

Lord Jesus, the gifts You have given us are different, according to the grace You have given. If my gift is prophesying, may I use it in proportion to my faith. If it is serving, may I serve; if it is teaching, may I teach; if it is encouraging, may I encourage; if it is contributing to the needs of others, may I give generously; if it is leadership, may I govern diligently; if it is showing mercy, may I do it cheerfully. By Your grace, Lord, I will be devoted to others in love. I will honor others above myself. I will never be lacking in zeal, but I will keep my spiritual fervor, serving You, Lord. I will share with God's people who are in need and practice hospitality.

🍃 PRAYERS, PRAISES, AND PERSONAL NOTES 🍃

_____

_____

_____

_____

_____

_____

Rom. 12:6-8, 10-11, 13 paraphrased, A Woman's Journey Toward Holiness, *186*

Be Spiritually Renewed

Forgiving Savior, I repent, change my mind and purpose; I turn around and return to You that my sins may be erased, blotted out, wiped clean, that times of refreshing may come from You. I will cleanse myself from all filthiness of the flesh and spirit, perfecting holiness in fear and reverence of You, O God. I will throw off my old evil nature and my former way of life, which is rotten through and through, full of lust and deception. Instead, I will be spiritually renewed in my thoughts and attitudes. I will display a new nature because I am like a new person, created in Your likeness, Lord—righteous, holy, and true.

🕯 PRAYERS, PRAISES, AND PERSONAL NOTES 🕯

_____

_____

_____

_____

_____

Acts 3:19 AMP; 2 Cor. 7:1b KJV; Eph. 4:22-24 NLT, all paraphrased,
A Woman's Journey Toward Holiness, 209

At Wits' End

"The mighty oceans have roared, O Lord. The mighty oceans roar like thunder; the mighty oceans roar as they pound the shore." "You have thrust me down to the lowest pit, into the darkest depths. Your anger lies heavy on me; wave after wave engulfs me." "Your waves and surging tides sweep over me." I reel and stagger like a drunken person; I am at my wits' end. I cry out to You, Lord, in my trouble; bring me out of my distress. O still the storm to a whisper, the waves of the sea to a hush. For mightier than the violent raging of the seas, mightier than the breakers on the shore, O Lord, You are mightier than these!

❧ PRAYERS, PRAISES, AND PERSONAL NOTES ❧

_____

_____

_____

_____

_____

Ps. 93:3 NLT; Ps. 88:6-7 NLT; Ps. 42:7b NLT not paraphrased; Ps. 107:27-29; Ps. 93:4 NLT paraphrased, A Woman's Pilgrimage of Faith, 16

Prepare Me for Service

As Your little child, Jesus, I will abide in You. I will lift up hands to Your Word, which I have loved; I will meditate and feed on Your Word. Now prepare me for works of service, so that Your body, Christ, may be built up. May the service that I perform not only supply the needs of God's people but also overflow in many expressions of thanks to You, O God. For I am looking to You, Jesus, the author and finisher of my faith. And I, with open face beholding as in a glass Your glory, Lord, am being changed into Your same image and likeness from glory to glory, even as by Your Spirit.

❧ PRAYERS, PRAISES, AND PERSONAL NOTES ❧

_____

_____

_____

_____

_____

_____

1 John 2:28a; Ps. 119:48 KJV; Eph. 4:12; 2 Cor. 9:12; Heb. 12:2a;
2 Cor. 3:18 KJV, all paraphrased, A Woman's Journey Toward Holiness, *212*

Co-Heir with Jesus

O my Hope, my Savior in times of distress, why are You like a stranger in the land, like a traveler who stays only a night? Why are You like a man taken by surprise, like a warrior powerless to save? You are with me, O Lord, and I bear Your name; do not forsake me! Now if I am Your child, then I am an heir—Your heir, O God, and co-heirs with You, Jesus, if indeed I share in Your sufferings in order that I may also share in Your glory. I consider that my present sufferings are not worth comparing with the glory that will be revealed in me. I glory in Your holy name; my heart seeks You, Lord, and rejoices.

PRAYERS, PRAISES, AND PERSONAL NOTES

_____

_____

_____

_____

_____

_____

Jer. 14:8-9; Rom. 8:17-18; Ps. 105:3, all paraphrased, A Woman's Pilgrimage of Faith, 18

Knowing Christ

O Lord, I bow down in worship; I kneel before You. For as I came from my mother's womb, I shall leave this world, naked as I came, and shall take nothing for my labor, which I may carry away in my hand. This also is a grievous evil: Just as I came, so shall I go; and what gain have I? I have labored for the wind. But I am confident, Lord, that everything You do will endure forever; nothing can be added to it, and nothing taken from it—so that I may revere You. "What is more, I consider everything a loss compared to the surpassing greatness of knowing Christ Jesus my Lord, for whose sake I have lost all things. I consider them rubbish, that I may gain Christ."

🌿 PRAYERS, PRAISES, AND PERSONAL NOTES 🌿

_____

_____

_____

_____

Ps. 95:6; Eccl. 5:15-16 RSV; Eccl. 3:14 paraphrased; Phil. 3:8 not paraphrased, A Woman's Pilgrimage of Faith, 21

To Love Is to Obey

Jesus, I pray that _____ will follow Your command: "Those who love God must also love their brothers and sisters." "Everyone who believes that Jesus is the Christ is God's child, and whoever loves the Father also loves the Father's children." So this is how they will know they love God's children: when they love You, God, and obey Your commands. Loving You means obeying Your commands. And Your commands are not too hard for them, "because everyone who is a child of God conquers the world. And this is the victory that conquers the world—our faith." Now help them win against the world because they believe that Jesus is the Son of God.

🌿 PRAYERS, PRAISES, AND PERSONAL NOTES 🌿

_____

_____

_____

_____

_____

1 John 4:21a paraphrased; 1 John 4:21b; 5:1 not paraphrased;
1 John 5:2-3 paraphrased; 1 John 5:4 not paraphrased; 1 John 5:5 paraphrased, all NCV

Let Me Not Be Put to Shame

"My God, my God, why have you forsaken me? Why are you so far from saving me, so far from the words of my groaning?" "Let me not be put to shame, O Lord, for I have cried out to you; but let the wicked be put to shame and lie silent in the grave." "Do not forsake me, O Lord; O my God, be not far from me!" "Draw near to me, redeem me, set me free." "I trust in you, O Lord; I say, 'You are my God.'"

🌿 PRAYERS, PRAISES, AND PERSONAL NOTES 🌿

_____

_____

_____

_____

_____

_____

_____

_____

_____

Ps. 22:1; Ps. 31:17; Ps. 38:21 NKJV; Ps. 69:18a NRSV; Ps. 31:14,
A Woman's Pilgrimage of Faith, 30

Rescue Me, Lord

O my Deliverer, "Turn your ear toward me. Rescue me quickly. Be a rock of refuge for me, a strong fortress to save me." "Pull me out of the mud; don't let me sink any deeper! Rescue me from those who hate me, and pull me from these deep waters." "O guard my life, and deliver me; do not let me be put to shame, for I take refuge in you." "Set me free from my prison, that I may praise your name. Then the righteous will gather about me because of your goodness to me."

🌿 PRAYERS, PRAISES, AND PERSONAL NOTES 🌿

_____

_____

_____

_____

_____

_____

_____

_____

Ps. 31:2 GOD'S WORD; Ps. 69:14 NLT; Ps. 25:20 NRSV; Ps. 142:7,
A Woman's Pilgrimage of Faith, 32

Bring Forth Fruit

Lord, I am blessed if I do not walk in the counsel of the ungodly, nor stand in the ways of sinners, nor sit in the seat of the mockers. My delight is in Your law, O Lord, and I will meditate on Your law day and night. Then I shall be like a tree planted by the rivers of water that brings forth fruit in season, whose leaf shall not wither. And whatsoever I do shall prosper. The ungodly are not so, but they are like the chaff which the wind blows away. Therefore ungodly people shall not stand in the judgment, nor sinners in the congregation of the righteous. Lord, You know the way of the righteous, but the way of the ungodly shall perish.

🌿 PRAYERS, PRAISES, AND PERSONAL NOTES 🌿

_____

_____

_____

_____

_____

_____

Ps. 1 KJV paraphrased

He Formed Me

"O my God, I cry by day, but you do not answer; and by night, but find no rest." "If I say, 'Surely the darkness shall cover me, and the light around me become night,' even the darkness is not dark to you; the night is as bright as the day, for darkness is as light to you. For it was you who formed my inward parts; you knit me together in my mother's womb." "From birth I was cast upon you; from my mother's womb you have been my God." Therefore, "I will lie down in peace and sleep, for you alone, O Lord, will keep me safe." "Lord, you have brought light to my life; my God, you light up my darkness."

PRAYERS, PRAISES, AND PERSONAL NOTES

_____

_____

_____

_____

_____

Ps. 22:2 NRSV; Ps. 139:11-13 NRSV; Ps. 22:10; Ps. 4:8 NLT; Ps. 18:28 NLT,
A Woman's Pilgrimage of Faith, 34

His Excellent Name

O Lord my Lord, how excellent is Your name in all the earth, who has set Your glory above the heavens! When I consider Your heavens, the work of Your fingers, the moon and the stars, which You have ordained, what am I that You are mindful of me, the child of my parents, or that You visit me? For You have made me a little lower than the angels and have crowned me with glory and honor. You have made me responsible for the works of Your hands; You have put all things under my feet: All sheep and oxen, yes, and the beasts of the field, the birds of the air, and the fish of the sea, and whatsoever passes through the paths of the seas. O Lord my Lord, how excellent is Your name in all the earth!

🌿 PRAYERS, PRAISES, AND PERSONAL NOTES 🌿

_____

_____

_____

_____

_____

Ps. 8:1, 3-9 KJV paraphrased

Stronghold in Trouble

Father God, "we looked for peace, but no good came; and for a time of health, and behold trouble!" You are good, O my Fortress, a stronghold in the day of trouble; and You know me, for I trust in You. Therefore, it's better that I am poor and walk in my integrity, than dishonest, perverse in speech, and a fool. "May integrity and uprightness protect me, because my hope is in you." "I will praise you forever for what you have done; in your name I will hope, for your name is good. I will praise you in the presence of your saints."

PRAYERS, PRAISES, AND PERSONAL NOTES

_____

_____

_____

_____

_____

_____

_____

Jer. 8:15 KJV not paraphrased; Nahum 1:7 KJV; Prov. 19:1 KJV paraphrased; Ps. 25:21; 52:9 not paraphrased, A Woman's Pilgrimage of Faith, 22

My Advocate on High

Even now, Lord, You are my witness in heaven, my Advocate on high, my Intercessor, and my Friend, as my eyes pour out tears to You. On my behalf plead with God as You plead for Your friends. Rescue me from my powerful enemy, from my foes, who are too strong for me. Hear my voice, O God, in my meditation; preserve my life from fear of the enemy.

PRAYERS, PRAISES, AND PERSONAL NOTES

_____

_____

_____

_____

_____

_____

_____

_____

_____

_____

Job 16:19-21; 2 Sam. 22:18; Ps. 64:1 NKJV, all paraphrased,
A Woman's Pilgrimage of Faith, 44

God's Reward

O Lord, You will reward me according to my righteousness; according to the cleanness of my hands You will reward me. Therefore, I will keep Your ways, Lord and will not wickedly depart from You, my God. For all Your judgments are before me, so I will not put away Your statutes from me. I will be upright before You, and I will keep myself from iniquity. Lord, You will reward me according to my righteousness, according to the cleanness of my hands in Your eyes. Yes, Lord, I will be merciful, and then You will show Yourself merciful; I will be upright; then You will show Yourself upright. I will be pure; then You will show Yourself pure.

PRAYERS, PRAISES, AND PERSONAL NOTES

_____

_____

_____

_____

_____

_____

Ps. 18:20-26a KJV paraphrased

His Hand of Blessing

O Christ, You are the mediator of a new covenant, that I who am called may receive the promised eternal inheritance—now that You have died as a ransom to set me free from my sins. Son of Man, You did not come to be served, but to serve, and to give Your life as a ransom for many. Therefore, "You do see! Indeed you note trouble and grief, that you may take it into your hands." "You both precede and follow me. You place your hand of blessing on my head. Such knowledge is too wonderful for me, too great for me to know!"

PRAYERS, PRAISES, AND PERSONAL NOTES

_____

_____

_____

_____

_____

_____

_____

Heb. 9:15; Matt. 20:28 paraphrased; Ps. 10:14a NRSV;
Ps. 139:5-6 NLT not paraphrased, A Woman's Pilgrimage of Faith, 196

Troubles of My Heart

O Silent One, "the troubles of my heart have multiplied; free me from my anguish." "I said to myself, 'I will watch what I do and not sin in what I say.'" "But as I stood there in silence—not even speaking of good things—the turmoil within me grew to the bursting point." "I am silent before you; I won't say a word." Through Your tender mercy, O God, by which You, the Dayspring from on high, have visited me, give light to me as I sit in darkness and in the shadow of death, to guide my feet into the way of peace. Then my heart will sing to You and not be silent. O Lord my God, I will give thanks to You forever.

🐾 PRAYERS, PRAISES, AND PERSONAL NOTES 🐾

_____

_____

_____

_____

_____

Ps. 25:17; Ps. 39:1a-2, 9a NLT not paraphrased; Luke 1:78-79 NKJV;
Ps. 30:12 paraphrased, A Woman's Pilgrimage of Faith, 33

The Heavens Tell of God's Glory

The heavens tell of Your glory, O God, and the skies announce what Your hands have made. "Day after day they tell the story; night after night they tell it again. They have no speech or words; they have no voice to be heard. But their message goes out through all the world; their words go everywhere on earth. The sky is like a home for the sun. The sun comes out like a bridegroom from his bedroom. It rejoices like an athlete eager to run a race. The sun rises at one end of the sky and follows its path to the other end. Nothing hides from its heat." "The earth belongs to the Lord, and everything in it— the world and all its people."

🕮 PRAYERS, PRAISES, AND PERSONAL NOTES 🕮

_____

_____

_____

_____

_____

_____

Ps. 19:1 paraphrased; Ps. 19:2-6; Ps. 24:1 not paraphrased, all NCV

Find Joy in God's Strength

I find joy in Your strength, O Lord, and in Your salvation I shall greatly rejoice! You have given me my heart's desire and have not withheld what I requested. For You presented me with the blessings of goodness. I asked life of You, and You gave it to me, even length of days forever and ever. Your glory is great in Your salvation; honor and majesty You have laid upon me. For You have made me most blessed forever; You have made me exceedingly glad in Your presence. Be exalted, O Lord, in Your own strength; I will sing and praise Your greatness.

🌿 PRAYERS, PRAISES, AND PERSONAL NOTES 🌿

_____

_____

_____

_____

_____

_____

_____

Ps. 21:1-3a, 4-6, 13 KJV paraphrased

Hope of Eternal Life

Ever-living God, I pray that _____
will not have sinful, unbelieving hearts that turn away
from You. I pray they will not become hardened by sin's
deceitfulness. Today, Jesus, I pray they will hear Your
voice. Keep them from hardening their hearts or becoming rebellious. May they have the faith of God's elect
and the knowledge of the truth that leads to godliness—
a faith and knowledge resting on the hope of eternal life
that You, who do not lie, promised from the beginning
of time.

❧ PRAYERS, PRAISES, AND PERSONAL NOTES ❧

_____

_____

_____

_____

_____

_____

_____

Heb. 3:12-13b, 15; Titus 1:1b-2, all paraphrased

The Lord Is My Shepherd

Lord, You are my shepherd; I shall not want. You make me to lie down in green pastures; You lead me beside the still waters. You restore my soul; You lead me in the paths of righteousness for Your name's sake. Yea, though I walk through the valley of the shadow of death, I will fear no evil, for You are with me. Your rod and Your staff, they comfort me. You prepare a table before me in the presence of my enemies; You anoint my head with oil; my cup runs over. Surely goodness and mercy shall follow me all the days of my life, and I will dwell in Your house forever.

PRAYERS, PRAISES, AND PERSONAL NOTES

Ps. 23 KJV paraphrased

Where Is God?

"All my longings lie open before you, O Lord; my sighing is not hidden from you." "My tears have been my food day and night, while they continually say to me, 'Where is your God?'" "My life is consumed by anguish and my years by groaning; my strength fails because of my affliction, and my bones grow weak." O Lord, let Your lovingkindness be upon me, according as I have hoped in You. Grant me Your peace, the peace of Your kingdom at all times and in all ways, under all circumstances and conditions, whatever comes. Lord, be with me.

❧ PRAYERS, PRAISES, AND PERSONAL NOTES ❧

_____

_____

_____

_____

_____

_____

_____

Ps. 38:9; Ps. 42:3 NKJV; Ps. 31:10 not paraphrased; Ps. 33:22 NAS95;
2 Thess. 3:16 AMP paraphrased, A Woman's Pilgrimage of Faith, 36

Show Me Your Ways

Unto You, O Lord, I lift up my soul. O my God, I trust in You; let me not be ashamed; let not my enemies triumph over me. Yes, let none that wait on You be ashamed; let them be ashamed that transgress without cause. Show me Your ways, O Lord; teach me Your paths. Good and upright are You, Lord; therefore, You will teach me, a sinner, the right way. The meek You will guide in judgment, and the meek You will teach Your way. All Your paths, Lord, are mercy and truth for me as I keep Your covenant and testimonies.

PRAYERS, PRAISES, AND PERSONAL NOTES

_____

_____

_____

_____

_____

_____

_____

Ps. 25:1-4, 8-10 KJV paraphrased

Do Not Forget Me, Lord

Arise, Lord! Lift up Your hand. Do not forget me, for I am helpless. "O Lord, how long will this go on? Will you hide yourself forever?" "How long must I wait? When will you punish those who persecute me?" "I am sick at heart. How long, O Lord, until you restore me?" "I weep with grief; encourage me by your word." "I am in trouble, so do not hide your face from me. Answer me quickly!" I truly trust in You, Lord. Because You, O God Most High, always love me, I will not be overwhelmed.

❧ PRAYERS, PRAISES, AND PERSONAL NOTES ❧

_____

_____

_____

_____

_____

_____

_____

Ps. 10:12 paraphrased; Ps. 89:46a NLT; Ps. 119:84 NLT; Ps. 6:3 NLT; Ps. 119:28 NLT; Ps. 69:17 GOD'S WORD not paraphrased; Ps. 21:7 NCV paraphrased, A Woman's Pilgrimage of Faith, 45

Turn, O Lord, and Deliver Me

"My soul is in anguish. How long, O Lord, how long?" Why do You hide Your face from me and forget my misery and oppression? You have walled me in so that I cannot escape; You have weighed me down with chains. "Turn, O Lord, and deliver me; save me because of your unfailing love." "I will exalt you, O Lord, for you lifted me out of the depths."

❧ PRAYERS, PRAISES, AND PERSONAL NOTES ❧

_____

_____

_____

_____

_____

_____

_____

_____

_____

_____

Ps. 6:3 not paraphrased; Ps. 44:24; Lam. 3:7 paraphrased;
Ps. 6:4; Ps. 30:1a not paraphrased, A Woman's Pilgrimage of Faith, 47

Beauty of Holiness

Lord, I give to You the glory due Your name; I worship You, Lord, in the beauty of holiness. Your voice is upon the waters; God of glory, You thunder; O Lord, You are upon many waters. Your voice is powerful; Your voice is full of majesty. Your voice breaks the cedars; yes, Lord, You break the cedars of Lebanon. Your voice divides the flames of fire. Your voice shakes the wilderness; You shake the wilderness of Kadesh. In Your temple everyone speaks of Your glory. O Lord, You sit enthroned upon the flood; yes, Lord, You are enthroned as king forever. Lord, You give strength to Your people; You bless Your people with peace.

PRAYERS, PRAISES, AND PERSONAL NOTES

_____

_____

_____

_____

_____

_____

Ps. 29:2-5, 7-8, 9b-11 KJV paraphrased

O Lord, Be My Helper!

"Listen to my cry for help, O God. Pay attention to my prayer." "My eyes fail from weeping, I am in torment within." "Have pity on me! O Lord, be my helper!" "O God, do not remain silent. Do not turn a deaf ear to me. Do not keep quiet, O God." "O Lord, listen to my prayer. Open your ears to hear my urgent requests. Answer me because you are faithful and righteous." "I call on you, O God, for you will answer me; give ear to me and hear my prayer."

PRAYERS, PRAISES, AND PERSONAL NOTES

_____

_____

_____

_____

_____

_____

_____

Ps. 61:1 GOD'S WORD; Lam. 2:11a; Ps. 30:10b GOD'S WORD; Ps. 83:1 GOD'S WORD; Ps. 143:1 GOD'S WORD; Ps. 17:6, A Woman's Pilgrimage of Faith, 46

His Amazing Ways

O Lord, "Hear the sound of my prayer, when I cry out to you for help. I raise my hands toward your Most Holy Place." "God, you will be praised in Jerusalem. We will keep our promises to you. You hear our prayers. All people will come to you. Our guilt overwhelms us, but you forgive our sins. Happy are the people you choose and invite to stay in your court. We are filled with good things in your house, your holy Temple. You answer us in amazing ways, God our Savior. People everywhere on the earth and beyond the sea trust you."

PRAYERS, PRAISES, AND PERSONAL NOTES

_____

_____

_____

_____

_____

_____

_____

Ps. 28:2; 65:1-5, all NCV

Strengthen My Heart

Grant me the desire of my heart and do not withhold the request of my lips. "Lord, don't be far away. You are my strength; hurry to help me." My bones are dried up, and my hope has perished. I am completely cut off. I wait in hope for You, Lord; You are my help and my shield. I'll be patient and wait on You; I'll be of good courage. O strengthen my heart, and I will wait patiently on You, Lord.

✦ PRAYERS, PRAISES, AND PERSONAL NOTES ✦

_____

_____

_____

_____

_____

_____

_____

_____

Ps. 21:2 paraphrased; Ps. 22:19 NCV not paraphrased; Ezek. 37:11b NAS95; Ps. 33:20;
Ps. 27:14 KJV paraphrased, A Woman's Pilgrimage of Faith, 50

Worship at God's Footstool

I will sing to You all my life, Lord; I will sing praise to You, my God, as long as I live. May my meditation be pleasing to You as I rejoice in You. I will constantly tell of all Your wonderful acts. I will glory in Your holy name; my heart seeks You and rejoices. "I thank and praise you, O God of my fathers." I exalt You and worship at Your footstool; You are holy. I worship You, Lord, in the splendor of Your holiness. Praise be to Your name forever and ever, for wisdom and power are yours.

🌿 PRAYERS, PRAISES, AND PERSONAL NOTES 🌿

_____

_____

_____

_____

_____

_____

_____

_____

Ps. 104:33-34; 105:2b, 3 paraphrased; Dan. 2:23a not paraphrased; Ps. 99:5; 96:9a; Dan. 2:20 paraphrased, A Woman's Walk with God, 156

My Soul Will Be Satisfied

"My heart is beaten down and withered like grass because I have forgotten about eating." "I eat ashes like bread and my tears are mixed with my drink." All my days I eat in darkness, and I have much sorrow and sickness and anger. O satisfy me early with Your mercy and unfailing love that I may rejoice and be glad all my days. Then "my soul will be satisfied as with the richest of foods; with singing lips my mouth will praise you."

PRAYERS, PRAISES, AND PERSONAL NOTES

_____

_____

_____

_____

_____

_____

_____

_____

Ps. 102:4, 9 GOD'S WORD not paraphrased; Eccl. 5:17 NKJV; Ps. 90:14 KJV paraphrased; Ps. 63:5 not paraphrased, A Woman's Pilgrimage of Faith, 49

Be a Peacemaker

May I have the wisdom, Lord, that comes from heaven, which is first of all pure, then peace-loving, considerate, submissive, full of mercy and good fruit, impartial and sincere. May I be a peacemaker, who by sowing in peace raises a harvest of righteousness. Help me to encourage others, so that we may build each other up. And I will respect those who work hard for You, Lord, who are over me in the Lord and who admonish me. I will hold them in the highest regard in love because of their work. I will live in peace with others. I will make sure that I do not pay back wrong for wrong, but I will always try to be kind to Christians and to everyone else.

☙ PRAYERS, PRAISES, AND PERSONAL NOTES ☙

_____

_____

_____

_____

James 3:17-18; 1 Thess. 5:11a, 12-13, all paraphrased,
A Woman's Journey Toward Holiness, 137

Losing My Life to Keep It

O my Security, if I try to make my life secure, I will lose it, but if I lose my life, I will keep it. "The truth is, a kernel of wheat must be planted in the soil. Unless it dies it will be alone—a single seed. But its death will produce many new kernels—a plentiful harvest of new lives." And if I love my life in this world, I will lose it. If I despise my life in this world, I will keep it for eternity.

PRAYERS, PRAISES, AND PERSONAL NOTES

_____

_____

_____

_____

_____

_____

_____

_____

_____

_____

Luke 17:33 NRSV paraphrased; John 12:24 NLT not paraphrased;
John 12:25 NLT paraphrased, A Woman's Pilgrimage of Faith, 61

Worry

O Lord of my Life, the world offers me only the lust for physical pleasure, the lust for everything I see, and pride in my possessions. These are not from You, Father. They are from this evil world. And this world is fading away, along with everything I crave. Therefore, Jesus, as You've instructed, I won't worry about everyday life—whether I have enough food, drink, and clothes. Life consists of more than food and clothing. I look at the birds. They don't need to plant or harvest or put food in barns because, heavenly Father, You feed them. And I am far more valuable to You than they are.

❧ PRAYERS, PRAISES, AND PERSONAL NOTES ❧

_____

_____

_____

_____

_____

_____

1 John 2:16-17a; Matt. 6:25-26, all NLT paraphrased, A Woman's Pilgrimage of Faith, 62

Trouble Is Near

Ever-caring Comforter, "The suffering you sent was good for me, for it taught me to pay attention to your principles." So "do not be far from me, for trouble is near and there is no one to help." Oh, that I may persevere and endure hardships for Your name and not grow weary. Strengthen me with all power according to Your glorious might so that I may have great endurance and patience. Now let this encourage me to endure persecution patiently and remain firm to the end, obeying Your commands and trusting in You, Jesus.

☙ PRAYERS, PRAISES, AND PERSONAL NOTES ☙

_____

_____

_____

_____

_____

_____

_____

Ps. 119:71 NLT; Ps. 22:11 not paraphrased; Rev. 2:3; Col. 1:11;
Rev. 14:12 NLT paraphrased, A Woman's Pilgrimage of Faith, 63

Heart of Compassion

Lord and Savior, "I know very well how foolish the message of the cross sounds to those who are on the road to destruction. But we who are being saved recognize this message as the very power of God." So I must never be ashamed to tell others about You, Lord. And I won't be ashamed of Christians either, even those in prison for You, Christ. With the strength You give me, I'll be ready to suffer with them for the proclamation of the Good News. So, as one who has been chosen by You, as one holy and beloved, I will put on a heart of compassion, kindness, humility, gentleness, and patience. I will set an example for the believers in speech, in life, in love, in faith, and in purity.

🌿 PRAYERS, PRAISES, AND PERSONAL NOTES 🌿

_____

_____

_____

_____

1 Cor. 1:18 NLT not paraphrased; 2 Tim. 1:8 NLT; Col. 3:12 NAS95;
1 Tim. 4:12b paraphrased, A Woman's Pilgrimage of Faith, 64

God Is Powerful

"Praise the Lord, God our Savior, who helps us every day. Our God is a God who saves us." "God, order up your power; show the mighty power you have used for us before." "Kingdoms of the earth, sing to God; sing praises to the Lord. Sing to the one who rides through the skies, which are from long ago. He speaks with a thundering voice. Announce that God is powerful. He rules over Israel, and his power is in the skies. God, you are wonderful in your Temple. The God of Israel gives his people strength and power. Praise God!"

🌿 PRAYERS, PRAISES, AND PERSONAL NOTES 🌿

_____

_____

_____

_____

_____

_____

_____

Ps. 68:19-20a, 28, 32-35 NCV

A Saving Shield

Your ways, O God, are without fault. Your words, Lord, are pure. You are a shield to _____, who trust in You. Who is God? Only the Lord. Who is the rock? Only our God. O God, You are their protection. Make their ways free from fault. Make them like deer that do not stumble, that can stand on the steep mountains. Protect them with Your saving shield. Support them with Your right hand. Stoop to make them great. Give them better ways to live so that they will live as You want them to.

🌿 PRAYERS, PRAISES, AND PERSONAL NOTES 🌿

_____

_____

_____

_____

_____

_____

_____

Ps. 18:30-33, 35-36 NCV paraphrased

The Place Where God Dwells

How lovely is the place where You dwell, O Lord of hosts! My soul longs, yes, even faints for Your courts; Lord, my heart and my flesh cry out for You, the living God. Yes, the sparrow has found a house, and the swallow a nest for herself, where she may lay her young, even near Your altars, O Lord of hosts, my King and my God. I am blessed that I dwell in Your house; I am still praising You. I am blessed because my strength is in You; I have set my heart on Your ways.

PRAYERS, PRAISES, AND PERSONAL NOTES

_____

_____

_____

_____

_____

_____

_____

_____

Ps. 84:1-5 KJV paraphrased

Sing a New Song

I will sing to You, Lord, a new song because You have done miracles. By Your right hand and holy arm You have won the victory. Lord, You have made known Your power to save; You have shown the other nations Your victory for Your people. You have remembered Your love and Your loyalty to your people. All the ends of the earth have seen Your power to save. "Shout with joy to the Lord, all the earth; burst into songs and make music. Make music to the Lord with harps, with harps and the sound of singing. Blow the trumpets and the sheep's horns; shout for joy to the Lord the King. Let the sea and everything in it shout; let the world and everyone in it sing. Let the rivers clap their hands; let the mountains sing together for joy."

❦ PRAYERS, PRAISES, AND PERSONAL NOTES ❧

_____

_____

_____

_____

Ps. 98:1-3 paraphrased; Ps. 98:4-8, not paraphrased, all NCV

Blessed

Jesus, You said that when I realize my need for You, I am blessed because the kingdom of heaven is mine. When I grieve and mourn, I am blessed because You will comfort me. When I am humble and meek, I am blessed because I will inherit the earth. When I hunger and thirst after righteousness, I am blessed because I will be filled. When I am merciful, I am blessed because I will obtain mercy. When I am pure in heart, I am blessed because I will see You, O God. When I am a peacemaker, I am blessed because I will be called Your child. When I am persecuted for righteousness' sake, I am blessed because the kingdom of heaven is mine. When people revile me and persecute me and say all manner of evil against me falsely, I am blessed for Your sake, O Lord. Therefore, I will rejoice and be exceedingly glad, for great is my reward in heaven.

PRAYERS, PRAISES, AND PERSONAL NOTES

_____

_____

_____

Matt. 5:3-12a KJV paraphrased

Keep My Loved Ones Safe

May the Lord now show my loved ones kindness and faithfulness, and I too will show them the same favor. Keep them safe, O God, for in You they take refuge. "You protect them by your presence from what people plan against them. You shelter them from evil words." May they live in the land and enjoy security. Guide them safely so they are unafraid, but may the sea engulf their enemies. For "the name of the Lord is a strong tower; the righteous run to it and are safe."

⚜ PRAYERS, PRAISES, AND PERSONAL NOTES ⚜

_____

_____

_____

_____

_____

_____

_____

2 Sam. 2:6a; Ps. 16:1 *paraphrased*; Ps. 31:20 NCV *not paraphrased*; Ps. 37:3b NRSV; Ps. 78:53 *paraphrased*; Prov. 18:10 *not paraphrased*, A Woman's Pilgrimage of Faith, 77

Stand Up for Me, O God

O Most High, "I have been banished from your sight." "My loved ones and my friends stand aloof from my plague, and my relatives stand afar off." "You have caused my companions to shun me; you have made me a thing of horror to them. I am shut in so that I cannot escape." "You must defend my innocence, O God, since no one else will stand up for me. You have closed their minds to understanding." Restore me, O God; make Your face shine upon me that I may be saved.

PRAYERS, PRAISES, AND PERSONAL NOTES

_____

_____

_____

_____

_____

_____

_____

_____

Jonah 2:4a; Ps. 38:11 NKJV; Ps. 88:8 NRSV; Job 17:3-4a NLT not paraphrased;
Ps. 80:3 paraphrased, A Woman's Pilgrimage of Faith, 79

His Unfailing Love Comforts Me

O ever-caring Lord, friends speak proudly, every one with neighbors; with flattering lips and with a double heart they speak to me. Lord, cut off all insincere lips and the tongue that speaks hurtful things. Rise up to rescue me, as I have longed for You to do. Lord, You will keep me safe; You will always protect me from such people. "Now let your unfailing love comfort me, just as you promised me, your servant. Surround me with your tender mercies so I may live."

❧ PRAYERS, PRAISES, AND PERSONAL NOTES ❧

_____

_____

_____

_____

_____

_____

_____

_____

Ps. 12:2-3 KJV; Ps. 12:5 NLT; Ps. 12:7 NCV paraphrased;
Ps. 119:76-77a NLT not paraphrased, A Woman's Pilgrimage of Faith, 81

The Lord's Plans

"There is no wisdom, no insight, no plan that can succeed against the Lord." "The Lord brings the counsel of the nations to nothing; he frustrates the plans of the peoples." Yes, Lord, "I know that you can do all things and that no plan of yours can be ruined." Therefore, I will commit my works to You, Lord, and my plans will be established. "I will hurry, without lingering, to obey your commands."

PRAYERS, PRAISES, AND PERSONAL NOTES

_____

_____

_____

_____

_____

_____

_____

_____

_____

Prov. 21:30; Ps. 33:10 NRSV; Job 42:2 NCV not paraphrased; Prov. 16:3 NAS95 paraphrased;
Ps. 119:60 NLT not paraphrased, A Woman's Pilgrimage of Faith, 80

Set My Feet on Solid Ground

Almighty God, "I have endured your terrors, and now I am in despair." "You have taken my loved ones and friends far away from me. Darkness is my only friend!" "Ruthless witnesses come forward. . . . They repay me evil for good and leave my soul forlorn." I am waiting patiently for You, Lord, to help me; turn to me and hear my cry. Lift me out of the pit of despair, out of the mud and the mire. Set my feet on solid ground and steady me as I walk along.

🌿 PRAYERS, PRAISES, AND PERSONAL NOTES 🌿

_____

_____

_____

_____

_____

_____

_____

Ps. 88:15b, 18 GOD'S WORD; Ps. 35:11a-12 not paraphrased;
Ps. 40:1-2 NLT paraphrased, A Woman's Pilgrimage of Faith, 82.

Be Slow to Get Angry

O Lord of Peace, I'll get rid of my bitterness, hot temper, anger, loud quarreling, cursing, and hatred. I'll be quick to listen, slow to speak, and slow to get angry, for my anger can never make things right in Your sight. I won't sin by letting anger gain control over me. I'll think about it overnight and remain silent. I'll think about the things that are good and worthy of praise. I'll think about the things that are true and honorable and right and pure and beautiful and respected.

🌿 PRAYERS, PRAISES, AND PERSONAL NOTES 🌿

_____

_____

_____

_____

_____

_____

_____

Eph. 4:31 GOD'S WORD; James 1:19-20 NLT; Ps. 4:4 NLT;
Phil. 4:8 NCV, all paraphrased, A Woman's Pilgrimage of Faith, 92

Cease from Anger

O God of Wisdom, "a fool gives full vent to anger, but the wise quietly holds it back." "One given to anger stirs up strife, and the hothead causes much transgression." Therefore, I will not be quickly provoked in my spirit. I will cease from anger and forsake wrath; I will not fret— it only causes harm. "Do not hide Your face from me; Do not turn Your servant away in anger; You have been my help; Do not leave me nor forsake me, O God of my salvation." For "Who is like you, O Lord, among the gods? Who is like you, majestic in holiness, awesome in splendor, doing wonders?"

❦ PRAYERS, PRAISES, AND PERSONAL NOTES ❦

_____

_____

_____

_____

_____

_____

Prov. 29:11, 22 NRSV not paraphrased; Eccl. 7:9a; Ps. 37:8 NKJV paraphrased;
Ps. 27:9 NKJV; Ex. 15:11 NRSV not paraphrased, A Woman's Pilgrimage of Faith, 93

Doorkeeper in God's House

O Lord God of hosts, hear my prayer; give ear, O God of Jacob. Behold, O God my shield, and look upon me, the one You anointed. For a day in Your courts is better than a thousand. I had rather be a doorkeeper in Your house, my God, than to dwell in the tents of wickedness. For, Lord God, You are a sun and shield; You give grace and glory; no good thing will You withhold from me if I walk uprightly. O Lord of hosts, I am blessed for trusting in You.

🔥 PRAYERS, PRAISES, AND PERSONAL NOTES 🔥

_____

_____

_____

_____

_____

_____

_____

_____

_____

Ps. 84:8-12 KJV paraphrased

Seek God's Precepts

Let Your mercies come to _____, O Lord. Then they will have an answer for those who reproach them, for they trust in Your Word. Do not keep Your word of truth from them when they speak, for they hope in Your judgments. I pray that they will keep Your law continually forever and ever. May they walk in liberty and seek Your precepts and speak of Your testimonies before the leaders of our country and not be ashamed.

🕮 PRAYERS, PRAISES, AND PERSONAL NOTES 🕮

_____

_____

_____

_____

_____

_____

_____

_____

_____

Ps. 119:41a-46 KJV paraphrased

Turn the Other Cheek

Lord Jesus, I am willing to listen to what You say. I will love my enemies. I will do good to those who hate me. I will pray for the happiness of those who curse me. I will pray for those who hurt me. If someone slaps me on one cheek, I will turn the other cheek. If someone demands my coat, I will offer my shirt also. I will give what I have to anyone who asks me for it, and when things are taken away from me, I won't try to get them back. I will do for others as I would like them to do for me. I will turn from evil and do good; I will seek peace and pursue it.

❧ PRAYERS, PRAISES, AND PERSONAL NOTES ❧

_____

_____

_____

_____

_____

_____

_____

Luke 6:27-31 NLT; Ps. 34:14, all paraphrased, A Woman's Pilgrimage of Faith, *94*

Walk in Newness of Life

Just as You, Christ, were raised from the dead by the glory of the Father, even so I also should walk in newness of life. For if I have been united with You, Jesus, in the likeness of Your death, certainly I also shall be in the likeness of Your resurrection. As a result, I can really know You and experience the mighty power that raised You from the dead. I can learn what it means to suffer with You, sharing in Your death. Praise be to God, the Father of my Lord Jesus Christ! In Your great mercy You have given me new birth into a living hope, through Jesus' resurrection from the dead.

PRAYERS, PRAISES, AND PERSONAL NOTES

_____

_____

_____

_____

_____

_____

Rom. 6:4b-5 NKJV; Phil. 3:10 NLT; 1 Peter 1:3, all paraphrased,
A Woman's Pilgrimage of Faith, 198

Love the Enemy

Ever-forgiving Lord, do I think I deserve credit merely for loving those who love me? Even the sinners do that! And if I do good only to those who do good to me, is that so wonderful? Even sinners do that much! I will love my enemies! I will do good to them, lend to them, and not be concerned that they might not repay. Then my reward from heaven will be very great, and I will truly be acting as Your child, O Most High. For You are kind to the unthankful and to those who are wicked. I must be compassionate just as You, Father, are compassionate.

PRAYERS, PRAISES, AND PERSONAL NOTES

_____

_____

_____

_____

_____

_____

Luke 6:32-33, 35-36 NLT, all paraphrased, A Woman's Pilgrimage of Faith, 95

God's Heavy Hand

"My complaint is still bitter today. I groan because God's heavy hand is on me." Lord, "stretch out your hand from on high; set me free." "Redeem me from human oppression, that I may keep your precepts." And I'll watch carefully so that no bitter root grows up to cause trouble and defile many. "My guilt is not hidden from you." I cannot see my own mistakes. Forgive me for my secret sins. Won't you restore my life again so that I may find joy in You?

✿ PRAYERS, PRAISES, AND PERSONAL NOTES ✿

_____

_____

_____

_____

_____

_____

_____

Job 23:2 NCV; Ps. 144:7a NRSV; Ps. 119:134 NRSV not paraphrased;
Heb. 12:15b paraphrased; Ps. 69:5b not paraphrased; Ps. 19:12 NCV;
Ps. 85:6 GOD'S WORD paraphrased, A Woman's Pilgrimage of Faith, 96

Mercy and Truth

Show us Your mercy, O Lord, and grant us Your salvation. We will listen to what You, O God, will speak; for You speak peace to your people and to your saints, but let us not turn again to folly. Surely Your salvation is near us who fear You, that Your glory may dwell in our land. Mercy and truth are joined together; righteousness and peace have kissed each other. Truth springs out of the earth, and righteousness looks down from heaven. Yes, Lord, You shall give that which is good, and our land shall yield her increase. Righteousness shall go before You and shall set us in the way of Your steps.

🐾 PRAYERS, PRAISES, AND PERSONAL NOTES 🐾

_____
_____
_____
_____
_____
_____
_____

Ps. 85:7-13 KJV paraphrased

Deliver Me from My Enemies

O God, "Those who are younger than I am laugh at me." "And now they make fun of me with songs. I have become a joke to them. Since they consider me disgusting, they keep their distance from me and don't hesitate to spit in my face. Because God has untied my cord and has made me suffer, they are no longer restrained in my presence. . . . They trip my feet and then prepare ways to destroy me." "My times are in your hand; deliver me from the hand of my enemies and persecutors." "You understand, O Lord; remember me and care for me." "O Lord my God, I take refuge in you; save and deliver me from all who pursue me."

🪶 PRAYERS, PRAISES, AND PERSONAL NOTES 🪶

_____

_____

_____

_____

_____

Job 30:1a, 9-11, 12b GOD'S WORD; Ps. 31:15 NRSV; Jer. 15:15a;
Ps. 7:1, A Woman's Pilgrimage of Faith, 97

Declare His Faithfulness

O righteous and just God, "Truth is nowhere to be found, and whoever shuns evil becomes a prey." "Furthermore, I have seen under the sun that in the place of justice there is wickedness and in the place of righteousness there is wickedness." And I am in bitterness of soul and pray to You, Lord, and weep in anguish. I will not hide Your righteousness within my heart; I will declare Your faithfulness and Your salvation. I will not conceal Your lovingkindness and Your truth from others. For "happy are those to whom the Lord imputes no iniquity, and in whose spirit there is no deceit."

🌿 PRAYERS, PRAISES, AND PERSONAL NOTES 🌿

_____

_____

_____

_____

_____

_____

Isa. 59:15a; Eccl. 3:16 NAS95 not paraphrased; 1 Sam. 1:10 NKJV; Ps. 40:10 KJV paraphrased; Ps. 32:2 NRSV not paraphrased, A Woman's Pilgrimage of Faith, 98

OCTOBER 10

Gain a Heart of Wisdom

"You, O God, have heard my vows; You have given me
the heritage of those who fear Your name." For the fear
of You, Lord, is the beginning of wisdom; all those who
practice it have a good understanding. Teach me to number my days aright that I may gain a heart of wisdom.

🌿 PRAYERS, PRAISES, AND PERSONAL NOTES 🌿

Ps. 61:5 NKJV not paraphrased; Ps. 111:10a NRSV; Ps. 90:12 paraphrased,
A Woman's Pilgrimage of Faith, 107

Always Remember

Jesus, I pray that _____ will always remember what they have been taught and not let go of it. Help them to keep all that they have learned; it is the most important thing in life. Help them avoid the ways of wicked people and not follow them. May they stay away from the wicked and keep on going, because these people cannot sleep until they do evil. They cannot rest until they harm someone. They feast on wickedness and cruelty as if they were eating bread and drinking wine. Instead may _____ follow the ways of good godly people, who are like the light of dawn, growing brighter and brighter until full daylight.

❧ PRAYERS, PRAISES, AND PERSONAL NOTES ❧

_____

_____

_____

_____

_____

_____

Prov. 4:13, 15-18 NCV paraphrased

Resist the Devil

Holy Spirit, You who dwell within me are greater than the evil one who is in this world. Your blood, Jesus Christ, cleanses me from all sin. Therefore, I'll discipline myself and keep alert. Like a roaring lion, my adversary the devil prowls around, looking for someone to devour. I submit myself, then, to You, O God. I resist the devil, and he must flee from me.

PRAYERS, PRAISES, AND PERSONAL NOTES

_____

_____

_____

_____

_____

_____

_____

_____

_____

1 John 4:4b; 1:7b NKJV; 1 Peter 5:8 NRSV; James 4:7, all paraphrased,
A Woman's Pilgrimage of Faith, 109

OCTOBER 13

He Prepared a Place for Me

Jesus, You most assuredly said to me that I who have heard Your Word and believed in God who sent You have everlasting life, and I shall not come into judgment, but I have passed from death into life. Therefore, I won't let my heart be troubled. I'll trust in You, God, and I'll trust in You, Jesus. There are many rooms in Your Father's house; You would not tell me this if it were not true. You went there to prepare a place for me. Since You prepared a place for me, You will come back and take me to be with You so that I may be where You are.

🔖 PRAYERS, PRAISES, AND PERSONAL NOTES 🔖

_____

_____

_____

_____

_____

_____

_____

John 5:24 NKJV; John 14:1-3 NCV, all paraphrased, A Woman's Pilgrimage of Faith, 110

Trust in the Lord

Lord, I was in trouble, so I called to You. You answered me and set me free. I will not be afraid because You are with me. People can't do anything to hurt me. Lord, You are with me to help me, so I will see my enemies defeated. It is better to trust in You, Lord, than to trust people. It is better to trust in You than to trust princes.

🌾 PRAYERS, PRAISES, AND PERSONAL NOTES 🌾

_____

_____

_____

_____

_____

_____

_____

_____

_____

_____

_____

Ps. 118:5-9 NCV paraphrased, A Woman's Pilgrimage of Faith, 111

My Refuge and Strength

O my Comforter, You are my refuge and strength, always ready to help in times of trouble. So I will not fear, even if earthquakes come and the mountains crumble into the sea. I who live in Your shelter, O Most High, will find rest in Your shadow, Almighty One. This I declare of You, Lord: You alone are my refuge, my place of safety; You are my God, and I am trusting You. You will shield me with Your wings. You will shelter me with Your feathers. Your faithful promises are my armor and protection.

PRAYERS, PRAISES, AND PERSONAL NOTES

_____

_____

_____

_____

_____

_____

_____

Ps. 46:1-2 NLT; Ps. 91:1-2, 4 NLT, all paraphrased, A Woman's Pilgrimage of Faith, 112

My Soul Thirsts for God

Lord God, "I stretch out my hands to you in prayer. Like parched land, my soul thirsts for you." "I am bowed down and brought very low; all day long I go about mourning." "The Lord has forsaken me, my Lord has forgotten me." "But God, who comforts the downcast, comforted us." "You are the God who saves me. All day long I put my hope in you." "With my mouth I will give thanks abundantly to the Lord; and in the midst of many I will praise Him."

PRAYERS, PRAISES, AND PERSONAL NOTES

Ps. 143:6 GOD'S WORD; *Ps. 38:6; Isa. 49:14b* NRSV; *2 Cor. 7:6a; Ps. 25:5b* NLT; *Ps. 109:30* NAS95, A Woman's Pilgrimage of Faith, *126*

Genuine Love

May Your unfailing love rest upon me, O Lord, even as I put my hope in You. Your divine power has given me everything I need for life and godliness through my knowledge of You, who called me by Your own glory and goodness. For this very reason, I will make every effort to add to my faith goodness; and to goodness, knowledge; and to knowledge, self-control; and to self-control, perseverance; and to perseverance, godliness. Godliness leads me to love other Christians, and finally I will grow to have genuine love for everyone. The more I grow like this, the more I will become productive and useful in my knowledge of You, Lord Jesus Christ.

❧ PRAYERS, PRAISES, AND PERSONAL NOTES ❧

_____

_____

_____

_____

_____

_____

Ps. 33:22; 2 Peter 1:3, 5-8 NLT, all paraphrased, A Woman's Pilgrimage of Faith, 127

Hope in His Name

Lord, Your plans stand firm forever. Your thoughts stand firm in every generation. Therefore, I will know and serve You with a single mind and willing heart, for You search my mind and understand my every plan and thought. Surely, Lord, I have a future ahead of me; my hope will not be disappointed. I know also that wisdom is sweet to my soul; if I find it, there is a future hope for me, and my hope will not be cut off. "I will praise you forever for what you have done; in your name I will hope, for your name is good. I will praise you in the presence of your saints."

🙠 PRAYERS, PRAISES, AND PERSONAL NOTES 🙢

_____

_____

_____

_____

_____

_____

Ps. 33:11 GOD'S WORD; 1 Chron. 28:9a NRSV; Prov. 23:18 NLT;
Prov. 24:14 paraphrased; Ps. 52:9 not paraphrased, A Woman's Pilgrimage of Faith, 128

Listen to My Cry for Mercy

"I cry out to you, O God, but you do not answer; I stand
up, but you merely look at me." "Why do you hide your
face and forget our misery and oppression?" "O Lord,
hear my prayer, listen to my cry for mercy; in your faithfulness and righteousness come to my relief." For "Your
righteousness is like the mighty mountains, your justice
like the ocean depths." "Keep back Your servant also
from presumptuous sins; let them not have dominion
over me. Then I shall be blameless, and I shall be innocent of great transgression."

❧ PRAYERS, PRAISES, AND PERSONAL NOTES ❧

_____

_____

_____

_____

_____

_____

_____

Job 30:20; Ps. 44:24; Ps. 143:1; Ps. 36:6a NLT; Ps. 19:13 NKJV,
A Woman's Pilgrimage of Faith, 129

Produce Only What Is Good

Light of the world, I pray that _____
will put aside the deeds of darkness and put on the
armor of light. For though their hearts were once full of
darkness, now they are full of light from You, Lord, and
their behavior should show it. For this light within produces only what is good and right and true. May they
try to find out what is pleasing to You and take no part
in the worthless deeds of evil and darkness; instead, may
they rebuke and expose these. Then true instruction will
be in their mouths, and nothing false will be found on
their lips. They will walk with You in peace and uprightness and turn many from sin.

🖈 PRAYERS, PRAISES, AND PERSONAL NOTES 🖈

_____

_____

_____

_____

_____

_____

Rom. 13:12b; Eph. 5:8-11 NLT; Mal. 2:6, all paraphrased

He Saw My Affliction

Remember me, O Lord; do not be exceedingly angry, and do not remember my iniquity forever. "What gain is there in my destruction, in my going down into the pit? Will the dust praise you? Will it proclaim your faithfulness?" "It is better to be of a lowly spirit among the poor than to divide the spoil with the proud." "I will be glad and rejoice in your love, for you saw my affliction and knew the anguish of my soul." I fear You, Lord, and will serve You in truth with all my heart; for I have considered what great things You have done for me.

❧ PRAYERS, PRAISES, AND PERSONAL NOTES ❧

_____

_____

_____

_____

_____

_____

_____

Isa. 64:9a NRSV paraphrased; Ps. 30:9; Prov. 16:19 NRSV; Ps. 31:7 not paraphrased; 1 Sam. 12:24 NKJV paraphrased, A Woman's Pilgrimage of Faith, 131

He Gave Me Life

Creator of Life, "'Your hands shaped and made me. Do you now turn around and destroy me? Remember that you molded me like a piece of clay. Will you now turn me back into dust?'" "You watched me as I was being formed in utter seclusion, as I was woven together in the dark of the womb." "You made all the delicate, inner parts of my body and knit me together in my mother's womb." "'You dressed me with skin and flesh; you sewed me together with bones and muscles. You gave me life and showed me kindness, and in your care you watched over my life.'"

PRAYERS, PRAISES, AND PERSONAL NOTES

_____

_____

_____

_____

_____

_____

Job 10:8-9 NCV; Ps. 139:13, 15 NLT; Job 10:11-12 NCV,
A Woman's Pilgrimage of Faith, 132

Lord, Help Me

"Lord, I call to you. Come quickly. Listen to me when I call to you. Let my prayer be like incense placed before you, and my praise like the evening sacrifice. Lord, help me control my tongue; help me be careful about what I say. Take away my desire to do evil or to join others in doing wrong. Don't let me eat tasty food with those who do evil. If a good person punished me, that would be kind. If he corrected me, that would be like perfumed oil on my head. I shouldn't refuse it. But I pray against those who do evil. Let their leaders be thrown down the cliffs. Then people will know that I have spoken correctly." "God, I look to you for help. I trust in you, Lord. Don't let me die. Protect me from the traps they set for me and from the net that evil people have spread. Let the wicked fall into their own nets, but let me pass by safely."

🐾 PRAYERS, PRAISES, AND PERSONAL NOTES 🐾

_____

_____

_____

Ps. 141:1-6, 8-10 NCV

Restore Me, Lord

Ever-loving Lord, "Even if I were right, my own mouth would say I was wrong; if I were innocent, my mouth would say I was guilty." "Correct me, Lord, but only with justice—not in your anger, lest you reduce me to nothing." "I hold fast to your statutes, O Lord; do not let me be put to shame." "I have taken refuge in you, O Lord. Never let me be put to shame. Save me because of your righteousness." Restore me to Yourself, O Lord, that I may be restored; renew my days as of old.

❧ PRAYERS, PRAISES, AND PERSONAL NOTES ❧

_____

_____

_____

_____

_____

_____

_____

_____

Job 9:20 NCV; Jer. 10:24; Ps. 119:31; Ps. 31:1 GOD'S WORD not paraphrased; Lam. 5:21 NRSV paraphrased, A Woman's Pilgrimage of Faith, 145

New Life in the Holy Spirit

"For the sake of your name, O Lord, forgive my iniquity, though it is great." For I desire to live according to my new life in the Holy Spirit. Then I won't be doing what my sinful nature craves. My old sinful nature loves to do evil, which is just the opposite to what You, Holy Spirit, want. And You give me desires that are opposite to what my sinful nature desires. These two forces are constantly fighting each other, and my choices are never free from this conflict. "But You, O God the Lord, deal with me for Your name's sake; because Your mercy is good, deliver me."

☙ PRAYERS, PRAISES, AND PERSONAL NOTES ❧

_____

_____

_____

_____

_____

_____

Ps. 25:11 not paraphrased; Gal. 5:16-17 NLT paraphrased; Ps. 109:21 NKJV not paraphrased,
A Woman's Pilgrimage of Faith, 146

Light That Leads to Life

Jesus, You are the light of the world. If I follow You, I won't be stumbling through the darkness, because I will have the light that leads to life. I repent now and turn to You, God, so that my sins may be wiped out, that times of refreshing may come from You. I will do what is right and come to the light gladly, so everyone can see that I am doing what You want. For, Jesus, You gave Your life to free me from every kind of sin, to cleanse me, and to make me Your very own, totally committed to doing what is right.

❧ PRAYERS, PRAISES, AND PERSONAL NOTES ❧

_____

_____

_____

_____

_____

_____

_____

John 8:12 NLT; Acts 3:19; John 3:21 NLT; Titus 2:14 NLT, all paraphrased,
A Woman's Pilgrimage of Faith, 147

Live for Christ

Lord Jesus, I eagerly expect and hope that I will in no way be ashamed, but will have sufficient courage so that now as always You will be exalted in my body, whether by life or by death. "For to me, to live is Christ and to die is gain. If I am to go on living in the body, this will mean fruitful labor for me. Yet what shall I choose? I do not know! I am torn between the two: I desire to depart and be with Christ, which is better by far; but it is more necessary . . . that I remain in the body." Therefore, whatever happens, I will conduct myself in a manner worthy of Your Gospel, O Christ.

⚜ PRAYERS, PRAISES, AND PERSONAL NOTES ⚜

_____

_____

_____

_____

_____

_____

Phil. 1:20 paraphrased; Phil. 1:21-24 not paraphrased; Phil. 1:27a paraphrased

Hidden Faults

Lord and Savior, "Tell me, what have I done wrong? Show me my rebellion and my sin. Why do you turn away from me? Why do you consider me your enemy? Would you terrify a leaf that is blown by the wind? Would you chase a dry stalk of grass? You write bitter accusations against me and bring up all the sins of my youth." "But who can detect their errors? Clear me from hidden faults." Restore me again, O God, and cause Your face to shine in pleasure and approval on me, and I shall be saved!

PRAYERS, PRAISES, AND PERSONAL NOTES

_____

_____

_____

_____

_____

_____

_____

*Job 13:23-26 NLT; Ps. 19:12 NRSV not paraphrased; Ps. 80:3 AMP paraphrased,
A Woman's Pilgrimage of Faith, 150*

Hope in His Unfailing Love

Ever-caring Lord, "I am scorned by all my enemies and despised by my neighbors—even my friends are afraid to come near me. When they see me on the street, they turn the other way. I have been ignored as if I were dead, as if I were a broken pot." "But I am trusting you, O Lord, saying, 'You are my God!'" "Return, O Lord, and rescue me. Save me because of your unfailing love." "Lord, don't hold back your tender mercies from me. My only hope is in your unfailing love and faithfulness."

❧ PRAYERS, PRAISES, AND PERSONAL NOTES ❧

_____

_____

_____

_____

_____

_____

_____

_____

Ps. 31:11-12, 14; Ps. 6:4; Ps. 40:11, all NLT, A Woman's Pilgrimage of Faith, *159*

Gentle Words

O Lord, the "tongue is a small thing, but what enormous damage it can do. A tiny spark can set a great forest on fire. And the tongue is a flame of fire. It is full of wickedness that can ruin your whole life. It can turn the entire course of your life into a blazing flame of destruction." "Sometimes it praises our Lord and Father, and sometimes it breaks out into curses against those who have been made in the image of God. And so blessing and cursing come pouring out of the same mouth." But "gentle words bring life and health." "Kind words are like honey—sweet to the soul and healthy for the body." Therefore, "I said to myself, 'I will watch what I do and not sin in what I say. I will curb my tongue.'"

🔉 PRAYERS, PRAISES, AND PERSONAL NOTES 🔉

_____

_____

_____

_____

James 3:5-6a, 9-10a; Prov. 15:4a; Prov. 16:24; Ps. 39:1a, all NLT,
A Woman's Pilgrimage of Faith, 160

Increase My Faith

Hear my prayer, O Lord, and give ear to my weeping; do not hold Your peace at my tears. For I will examine myself, making sure my faith is genuine, proving and testing my own self. I won't profess that I know You and then in words and actions deny You. Lord, I ask You now to increase my faith.

❧ PRAYERS, PRAISES, AND PERSONAL NOTES ❧

_____

_____

_____

_____

_____

_____

_____

_____

_____

_____

Ps. 39:12a; 2 Cor. 13:5a; Titus 1:16a; Luke 17:5, all KJV paraphrased,
A Woman's Pilgrimage of Faith, 161

Show Mercy

Yes, Lord, I will continue to build my life on the foundation of my holy faith and to pray as I am directed by the Holy Spirit. I'll show mercy to those whose faith is wavering. I will encourage others and build them up. I'll show by my good life that my works are done with gentleness born of wisdom. And now all glory to You, Lord, who are able to keep me from stumbling and who will bring me into Your glorious presence innocent of sin and with great joy.

❧ PRAYERS, PRAISES, AND PERSONAL NOTES ❧

_____

_____

_____

_____

_____

_____

_____

_____

Jude 20, 22 NLT; 1 Thess. 5:11a; James 3:13b NRSV; Jude 24 NLT, all paraphrased,
A Woman's Pilgrimage of Faith, 164

Meditate on All God's Works

O kind and loving Lord, satisfy _____
in the morning with Your unfailing love so that they will
sing for joy and be glad all their days. "Remember, O
Lord, Your great mercy and love, for they are from of
old." I pray they will remember Your deeds, Lord; yes,
cause them to remember Your miracles of long ago and
to meditate on all Your works and consider all Your
mighty deeds. May they acknowledge You, O God, and
serve You with wholehearted devotion and willing
minds, for You search their hearts and understand every
motive behind their thoughts.

✤ PRAYERS, PRAISES, AND PERSONAL NOTES ✤

_____

_____

_____

_____

_____

_____

Ps. 90:14 paraphrased; Ps. 25:6 not paraphrased; Ps. 77:11-12; 1 Chron. 28:9a paraphrased

Encourage My Heart, O Lord

O my Deliverer, "I have become the ridicule of all my people—their taunting song all the day." "God has made my name a curse word; people spit in my face. My sight has grown weak because of my sadness, and my body is as thin as a shadow." "I am poor and helpless; God, hurry to me. You help me and save me. Lord, do not wait." Surely You will listen to my cry and comfort me. Now, Lord Jesus Christ and God my Father, who loved me and by Your grace gave me eternal encouragement and good hope, encourage my heart and strengthen me.

PRAYERS, PRAISES, AND PERSONAL NOTES

_____

_____

_____

_____

_____

_____

_____

Lam. 3:14 NKJV; Job 17:6-7 NCV; Ps. 70:5 NCV not paraphrased; Ps. 10:17b NLT;
2 Thess. 2:16-17a paraphrased, A Woman's Pilgrimage of Faith, 66

Faithful Servants

I thank You, God, upon every remembrance of your faithful servants. Always in every prayer of mine for all of them I make my requests with joy, for their fellowship in the Gospel from the first day until now. Being confident of this very thing, that You who have begun a good work in them will perform it until the day of Jesus Christ. It is right for me to think this of them because I have them in my heart. And I thank You, Christ Jesus my Lord, for Your servants that You consider to be faithful, appointing them to minister and serve You.

PRAYERS, PRAISES, AND PERSONAL NOTES

_____

_____

_____

_____

_____

_____

_____

Phil. 1:3-7a; 1 Tim. 1:12, all KJV paraphrased

Be Strong and Courageous

Almighty Protector, You have commanded me: "Be strong and courageous; do not be frightened or dismayed, for the Lord your God is with you wherever you go." "So we can say with confidence, 'The Lord is my helper; I will not be afraid. What can anyone do to me?'" And, Jesus, I will remember, You are with me always, to the end of the age.

🌿 PRAYERS, PRAISES, AND PERSONAL NOTES 🌿

_____

_____

_____

_____

_____

_____

_____

_____

_____

Josh. 1:9b NRSV; Heb. 13:6 NRSV not paraphrased; Matt. 28:20b NRSV paraphrased,
A Woman's Pilgrimage of Faith, 178

Forsake Me Not, O Lord

O Lord, I am facing so many uncertainties. For You have blocked my way so I cannot pass; You have shrouded my paths in darkness. You have made my heart faint; Almighty God, You have terrified me. "When I looked for good, then evil came to me; when I waited for light, there came darkness." "Forsake me not, O Lord; O my God, be not far from me." Be my strength, for I am poor; be my refuge and strength, for I am needy in my distress; be my shelter from the storm and a shade from the heat. I am casting my burdens on You, Lord, and releasing the weight of them to You, for You will sustain me.

🌾 PRAYERS, PRAISES, AND PERSONAL NOTES 🌾

_____

_____

_____

_____

_____

Job 19:8; 23:16 paraphrased; Job 30:26 AMP; Ps. 38:21 AMP not paraphrased; Isa. 25:4a KJV; Ps. 55:22a AMP paraphrased, A Woman's Journey Toward Holiness, 85

Transformed into His Likeness

Now, Lord, You are the Spirit, and where the Spirit of the Lord is, there is freedom. And I, who with an unveiled face reflect Your glory, Lord, am being transformed into Your likeness with ever-increasing glory, which comes from You, Lord, who are the Spirit. For my citizenship is in heaven, from which I also eagerly wait for You, my Savior, Lord Jesus Christ, who will transform my lowly body that it may be conformed to Your glorious body, according to the working by which You are able even to subdue all things to Yourself. All glory to You, who alone are God my Savior, through Jesus Christ my Lord. Yes, glory, majesty, power, and authority belong to You in the beginning, now, and forevermore. Amen.

☞ PRAYERS, PRAISES, AND PERSONAL NOTES ☜

_____

_____

_____

_____

2 Cor. 3:17-18; Phil. 3:20-21 NKJV; Jude 25 NLT, all paraphrased,
A Woman's Pilgrimage of Faith, 180

Abide in His Love

O Love eternal, I have known and believed the love that You have for me. God, You are love, and I who abide in love abide in You, O God, and You in me. Love has been perfected in me in this: that I may have boldness in the day of judgment; because as You are, so am I in this world. Yes, Jesus, I love You because You first loved me.

❧ PRAYERS, PRAISES, AND PERSONAL NOTES ❧

_____

_____

_____

_____

_____

_____

_____

_____

_____

_____

1 John 4:16-17, 19 NKJV paraphrased, A Woman's Pilgrimage of Faith, 181

Mighty Inner Strength

O Lord, I pray that from Your glorious, unlimited resources You will give me mighty inner strength through Your Holy Spirit. And I pray that, Christ, You will be more and more at home in my heart as I trust in You. May my roots go down deep into the soil of Your marvelous love. And may I have the power to understand, as all God's people should, how wide, how long, how high, and how deep Your love really is. May I experience Your love, Christ, though it is so great I will never fully understand it. Then I will be filled with the fullness of life and power that comes from You. Now glory be to You, Lord! By Your mighty power at work within me, You are able to accomplish infinitely more than I would ever dare to ask or hope.

PRAYERS, PRAISES, AND PERSONAL NOTES

_____

_____

_____

_____

Eph. 3:16-20 NLT paraphrased, A Woman's Pilgrimage of Faith, 182

Wash Away My Guilt

Ever-forgiving Savior, "Wash away all my guilt and make me clean again." "For I recognize my shameful deeds—they haunt me day and night." "You spread out our sins before you—our secret sins—and you see them all." "You are the only one I have sinned against; I have done what you say is wrong. You are right when you speak and fair when you judge." "You want me to be completely truthful, so teach me wisdom. Take away my sin, and I will be clean. Wash me, and I will be whiter than snow."

✍ PRAYERS, PRAISES, AND PERSONAL NOTES ✍

_____

_____

_____

_____

_____

_____

_____

Ps. 51:2 NCV; Ps. 51:3 NLT; Ps. 90:8 NLT; Ps. 51:4, 6-7 NCV,
A Woman's Pilgrimage of Faith, 148

The Good Shepherd

Jesus, You are the Good Shepherd. As such You lay down Your life for the sheep. "The hired hand is not the shepherd who owns the sheep. So when he sees the wolf coming, he abandons the sheep and runs away. Then the wolf attacks the flock and scatters it. The man runs away because he is a hired hand and cares nothing for the sheep." Jesus, my Good Shepherd, You know me, and I know You—just as the Father knows You and You know the Father—and You lay down Your life for me.

🕯 PRAYERS, PRAISES, AND PERSONAL NOTES 🕯

_____

_____

_____

_____

_____

_____

_____

John 10:11 paraphrased; 10:12-13 not paraphrased; 10:14-15 paraphrased,
A Woman's Pilgrimage of Faith, 183

God Is My Rock

"When I said, 'My foot is slipping,' your love, O Lord, supported me. When anxiety was great within me, your consolation brought joy to my soul." For "The Lord is my rock, my fortress and my deliverer; my God is my rock, in whom I take refuge. He is my shield and the horn of my salvation, my stronghold." "As for God, his way is perfect; the word of the Lord is flawless. He is a shield for all who take refuge in him. For who is God besides the Lord? And who is the Rock except our God? It is God who arms me with strength and makes my way perfect." "Surely God is my help; the Lord is the one who sustains me."

🍂 PRAYERS, PRAISES, AND PERSONAL NOTES 🍂

Ps. 94:18-19; Ps. 18:2, 30-32; Ps. 54:4, *A Woman's Pilgrimage of Faith, 184*

Furnace of Adversity

Sovereign Lord, You have refined me, but not like silver; You have tested me in the furnace of adversity. Therefore, I will keep alert, stand firm in my faith, be courageous and strong. How much better to get wisdom than gold, to choose understanding rather than silver! Now may I always be filled with the fruit of Your salvation—those good things that are produced in my life by You, Jesus Christ—for this will bring much glory and praise to You, O God.

PRAYERS, PRAISES, AND PERSONAL NOTES

_____

_____

_____

_____

_____

_____

_____

_____

Isa. 48:10 NRSV; 1 Cor. 16:13 NRSV; Prov. 16:16; Phil. 1:11 NLT, all paraphrased,
A Woman's Pilgrimage of Faith, 195

Holy Spirit, Pray for Me

Jesus Christ, the Righteous One, if I sin, I have You who will speak to the Father in my defense. Therefore, O God, You are able once and forever to save me. I come to You through Christ Jesus, for He lives forever to plead with You on my behalf. And, Holy Spirit, You help me in my distress. For I don't even know what I should pray for, nor how I should pray. But You pray for me with groanings that I cannot express in words. And, Father, You who know my heart know what the Holy Spirit is saying, for He pleads for me in harmony with Your own will.

PRAYERS, PRAISES, AND PERSONAL NOTES

_____

_____

_____

_____

_____

_____

1 John 2:1b; Heb. 7:25 NLT; Rom. 8:26-27 NLT, all paraphrased,
A Woman's Pilgrimage of Faith, 199

A Time for Everything

God of Justice, "I said to myself, 'In due season God will judge everyone, both good and bad, for all their deeds.'" "Those who obey him will not be punished. Those who are wise will find a time and a way to do what is right. Yes, there is a time and a way for everything, even as people's troubles lie heavily upon them. Indeed, how can people avoid what they don't know is going to happen? None of us can hold back our spirit from departing. None of us has the power to prevent the day of our death." Precious in Your sight, O Lord, is the death of Your saints. Yes, Jesus, You have gone to prepare a place for us, and You will come again and receive us unto Yourself, that where You are, there we may be also.

🌺 PRAYERS, PRAISES, AND PERSONAL NOTES 🌺

_____

_____

_____

_____

_____

Eccl. 3:17; 8:5-8a NLT not paraphrased; Ps. 116:15 KJV; John 14:3 KJV paraphrased

I Love You, Lord

O my Shepherd, I am Yours, a sheep of Your flock. I will thank You always; forever and ever I will praise You. "I love you, O Lord, my strength." I love You, Lord my God, with all my heart and with all my soul and with all my mind and with all my strength. And I will love my neighbor as myself. There are no commandments greater than these to love God and man.

PRAYERS, PRAISES, AND PERSONAL NOTES

_____

_____

_____

_____

_____

_____

_____

_____

_____

_____

Ps. 79:13 NCV paraphrased; Ps. 18:1 not paraphrased; Mark 12:30-31 paraphrased,
A Woman's Pilgrimage of Faith, 162

Perfecting Holiness

Hear, O Holy Lord, when I cry with my voice. Have mercy upon me, answer me, and help me. When You said, "Seek My face," my heart said to You, "Your face, Lord, will I seek." And I will purify myself from everything that contaminates my body and spirit, perfecting holiness out of reverence for You. I will flee evil desires and pursue righteousness, faith, love, and peace, along with those who call on You, Lord, out of a pure heart. I glory in Your holy name; I seek You, and my heart rejoices. I seek You, Lord, and Your strength; I will seek Your face forevermore.

🌿 PRAYERS, PRAISES, AND PERSONAL NOTES 🌿

_____

_____

_____

_____

_____

_____

Ps. 27:7-8 KJV; 2 Cor. 7:1; 2 Tim. 2:22; Ps. 105:3-4, all paraphrased,
A Woman's Journey Toward Holiness, 23

Renewed by the Holy Spirit

O God my Savior, when Your kindness and love appeared, You saved me, not because of righteous things I had done, but because of Your mercy. You saved me through the washing of rebirth and renewal by the Holy Spirit, whom You poured out on me generously through Jesus Christ my Savior. I have begun to live the new life, in which I am being made new and am becoming like the one who made me. This new life brings me the true knowledge of You, O God. For my hope is in You, Lord, who will renew my strength.

PRAYERS, PRAISES, AND PERSONAL NOTES

_____

_____

_____

_____

_____

_____

_____

Titus 3:4-6; Col. 3:10 NCV; Isa. 40:31a, all paraphrased,
A Woman's Pilgrimage of Faith, 179

Finish the Race

Jesus, I'll remember that in a race everyone runs, but only one person gets the prize. I also must run in such a way that I will win. I will consider it pure joy whenever I face trials of many kinds, because I know that the testing of my faith develops perseverance. Perseverance must finish its work so that I may be mature and complete, not lacking anything. Then I can say, "I have fought a good fight, I have finished the race, and I have remained faithful. And now the prize awaits me—the crown of righteousness that the Lord, the righteous Judge, will give me on that great day of his return. And the prize is not just for me but for all who eagerly look forward to his glorious return."

🪶 PRAYERS, PRAISES, AND PERSONAL NOTES 🪶

_____

_____

_____

_____

1 Cor. 9:24 NLT; James 1:2-4; paraphrased; 2 Tim. 4:7-8 NLT not paraphrased,
A Woman's Pilgrimage of Faith, 194

God's Servants

O God, empower _____ to preach the Word; to be prepared in season and out of season; to correct, rebuke, and encourage—with great patience and careful instruction. When they speak, I pray You will give them words so that they can tell the secret of the Good News without fear. Grant them strength to control themselves at all times, accept troubles, do the work of telling the Good News, and complete all the duties of a servant of God. Now I pray they will be careful for themselves and for all the people the Holy Spirit has given to them to care for. They must be like shepherds to the church of God, which You bought with the death of Your own Son.

⚘ PRAYERS, PRAISES, AND PERSONAL NOTES ⚘

_____

_____

_____

_____

_____

2 Tim. 4:2; Eph. 6:19 NCV; 2 Tim. 4:5 NCV; Acts 20:28 NCV, *all paraphrased*

Praise God's Awesome Name

Glorious God of heaven, You are in Your holy temple; You are on Your heavenly throne. Who is like You, the One who sits enthroned on high, who stoops down to look on the heavens and the earth? Living Lord, I exalt You and worship at Your footstool; You are holy. I praise Your great and awesome name, for You are holy. There is no one holy like You; there is no one beside You. O Holy One, I will praise Your name, for Your name alone is exalted; Your splendor is above the earth and the heavens.

❧ PRAYERS, PRAISES, AND PERSONAL NOTES ❧

_____

_____

_____

_____

_____

_____

_____

Ps. 11:4a; 113:5-6; 99:5, 3; 1 Sam. 2:2a; Ps. 148:13, all paraphrased,
A Woman's Journey Toward Holiness, 26

Give Thanks to the Lord

It is good to give thanks unto You, Lord, and to sing praises to Your name, O most High, to demonstrate Your lovingkindness in the morning and Your faithfulness every night. For You make me glad by Your works; I will sing for joy because of the works of Your hands. Therefore, I will give thanks to You, O Lord, among the people, and I will sing praises to Your name. To You, O God, I give thanks, to You I give thanks; for Your name is near, as Your wondrous works declare.

PRAYERS, PRAISES, AND PERSONAL NOTES

_____

_____

_____

_____

_____

_____

_____

_____

Ps. 92:1-2, 4; 2 Sam. 22:50; Ps. 75:1, all KJV paraphrased

How Majestic Is His Name

"O Lord, our Lord, how majestic is your name in all the earth! You have set your glory above the heavens." I will glory in Your holy name; my heart seeks You, Lord, and rejoices. I will sing to the glory of Your name; I will make Your praise glorious! "Who will not fear you, O Lord, and bring glory to your name? For you alone are holy. All nations will come and worship before you, for your righteous acts have been revealed." Blessed are You, King Jesus, who comes in the name of the Lord; peace in heaven, and glory in the highest!

❧ PRAYERS, PRAISES, AND PERSONAL NOTES ❧

_____

_____

_____

_____

_____

_____

_____

Ps. 8:1 not paraphrased; 1 Chron. 16:10; Ps. 66:2 paraphrased; Rev. 15:4 not paraphrased; Luke 19:38 KJV paraphrased, A Woman's Journey Toward Holiness, 200

Sacrifice of Praise

Lord Jesus, I will sacrifice a thank offering to You and call on Your name. Through You I will offer a sacrifice of praise to God continually, that is, the fruit of my lips giving thanks to Your name. I will sacrifice a freewill offering to You, Lord; I will praise Your name, for it is good. For You have delivered me from all my troubles. I will offer the sacrifices of thanksgiving and rehearse Your deeds with shouts of joy and singing!

PRAYERS, PRAISES, AND PERSONAL NOTES

_____

_____

_____

_____

_____

_____

_____

_____

_____

Ps. 116:17; Heb. 13:15 KJV; Ps. 54:6-7a; Ps. 107:22 AMP, all paraphrased,
A Woman's Journey Toward Holiness, 201

Enter His Gates with Thanksgiving

Lord, with all the earth I make a joyful sound to You. I serve You with gladness! I come into Your presence with singing! I know, Lord, that You are God! It is You who made me, and I am yours. I belong to You; I am a sheep of Your pasture. I enter Your gates with thanksgiving and Your courts with praise! I give thanks to You and bless Your name! For You are good, and Your steadfast love endures forever, and Your faithfulness to all generations. Praise You, Lord. Praise You for Your mighty deeds; praise You for Your exceeding greatness!

PRAYERS, PRAISES, AND PERSONAL NOTES

_____

_____

_____

_____

_____

_____

_____

Ps. 100; 150:1a-2 RSV paraphrased, A Woman's Walk with God, 113

Come with Thanksgiving

"God, we thank you; we thank you because you are near. We tell about the miracles you do." "You make the grass for cattle and vegetables for the people. You make food grow from the earth." "All living things look to you for food, and you give it to them at the right time." You give food to every living creature. Your love continues forever. We give thanks to You, God of heaven. We come to You with thanksgiving. Praise You, Lord! Thank You, Lord, because You are good. Your love continues forever.

🔖 PRAYERS, PRAISES, AND PERSONAL NOTES 🔖

Ps. 75:1; 104:14; 145:15 NCV not paraphrased;
Ps. 136:25-26a; 95:2a; 106:1 NCV paraphrased

A Bountiful Harvest

Our Creator, You formed the mountains by your power and armed yourself with mighty strength. You quieted the raging oceans with their pounding waves and silenced the shouting of the nations. Those who live at the ends of the earth stand in awe of your wonders. . . . You take care of the earth and water it, making it rich and fertile. The rivers of God will not run dry; they provide a bountiful harvest of grain, for you have ordered it so. You drench the plowed ground with rain, melting the clods and leveling the ridges. You soften the earth with showers and bless its abundant crops. You crown the year with a bountiful harvest. . . . The wilderness becomes a lush pasture, and the hillsides blossom with joy. The meadows are clothed with flocks of sheep, and the valleys are carpeted with grain. They all shout and sing for joy!"

🌾 PRAYERS, PRAISES, AND PERSONAL NOTES 🌾

_____

_____

_____

Ps. 65:6–13 NLT

Be Thankful

"Praise the Lord! Sing a new song to the Lord; sing his praise in the meeting of his people." "Let those who worship him rejoice in his glory." I will worship You, Son of God, in the splendor of Your holiness; may all the earth tremble before You. I worship You with gladness and come before You with joyful songs. Since I am receiving a kingdom that cannot be shaken, I will be thankful, and so worship You, God, acceptably with reverence and awe.

PRAYERS, PRAISES, AND PERSONAL NOTES

_____

_____

_____

_____

_____

_____

_____

_____

Ps. 149:1, 5a NCV not paraphrased; Ps. 96:9; 100:2; Heb. 12:28 paraphrased

Holy, Holy, Holy Is the Lord

"'Holy, holy, holy is the Lord God Almighty, who was, and is, and is to come.'" Great are You, Lord, and most worthy of praise, in the city of my God, Your holy mountain. You are the Mighty One, O God, the Lord, who speaks and summons the earth from the rising of the sun to the place where it sets. Gracious are You, Lord, and righteous; yes, my God is merciful. My mouth will speak in praise of You, Lord. Let every creature praise Your holy name forever and ever.

PRAYERS, PRAISES, AND PERSONAL NOTES

_____

_____

_____

_____

_____

_____

_____

_____

Rev. 4:8b not paraphrased; Ps. 48:1; 50:1; Ps. 116:5 KJV; Ps. 145:21 paraphrased,
A Woman's Journey Toward Holiness, 214

Praise the Lord!

"Praise the Lord! Praise God in his Temple; praise him in his mighty heaven. Praise him for his strength; praise him for his greatness. Praise him with trumpet blasts; praise him with harps and lyres. Praise him with tambourines and dancing; praise him with stringed instruments and flutes. Praise him with loud cymbals; praise him with crashing cymbals. Let everything that breathes praise the Lord. Praise the Lord!"

PRAYERS, PRAISES, AND PERSONAL NOTES

_____

_____

_____

_____

_____

_____

_____

_____

Ps. 150 NCV

Clothed with Compassion

"Sing for joy, O heavens, and exult, O earth; break forth, O mountains, into singing! For the Lord has comforted his people, and will have compassion on his suffering ones." "Blessed be the Lord, for He has shown me His marvelous kindness!" "This is my comfort in my distress, that your promise gives me life." Therefore, O God, as Your chosen one, holy and dearly loved, I will clothe myself with compassion, kindness, humility, gentleness, and patience.

PRAYERS, PRAISES, AND PERSONAL NOTES

_____

_____

_____

_____

_____

_____

_____

Isa. 49:13 NRSV; Ps. 31:21 NKJV; Ps. 119:50 NRSV not paraphrased; Col. 3:12 paraphrased, A Woman's Pilgrimage of Faith, 212

Anxious Hearts

O Prince of Peace, anxious hearts weigh _____
down. Help them to banish anxiety from their hearts
and cast off the troubles of their bodies. Remind them
to cast all their anxieties on You because You care for
them. Deliver them from worrying about tomorrow, for
tomorrow will worry about itself. Each day has enough
trouble of its own. When anxiety is great within them,
may Your consolation bring joy to their souls. May Your
grace and peace be with them.

🪶 PRAYERS, PRAISES, AND PERSONAL NOTES 🪶

_____

_____

_____

_____

_____

_____

_____

_____

Prov. 12:25a; Eccl. 11:10a; 1 Peter 5:7; Matt. 6:34; Ps. 94:19; Col. 1:2b paraphrased

No Other Name

You are the Lord. You have called me in righteousness. You have taken me by the hand and kept me; You have given me as a covenant to the people, a light to the nations, to open the eyes that are blind, to bring out the prisoners from the dungeon and from the prison those who sit in darkness. "This is right and is acceptable in the sight of God our Savior, who desires everyone to be saved and to come to the knowledge of the truth." For "'There is salvation in no one else! There is no other name in all of heaven for people to call on to save them.'"

🌿 PRAYERS, PRAISES, AND PERSONAL NOTES 🌿

_____

_____

_____

_____

_____

_____

Isa. 42:6-7 NRSV paraphrased; 1 Tim. 2:3-4 NRSV; Acts 4:12 NLT not paraphrased,
A Woman's Pilgrimage of Faith, 214

Equip Me

Ever-giving Lord, I must be an example to others by doing good deeds of every kind. May I learn to maintain good works, to meet urgent needs, that I may not be unfruitful. Equip me with everything good for doing Your will, and may You work in me what is pleasing to You, through Jesus Christ, to whom be glory forever and ever. Amen.

PRAYERS, PRAISES, AND PERSONAL NOTES

_____

_____

_____

_____

_____

_____

_____

_____

_____

_____

Titus 2:7a NLT; Titus 3:14 NKJV; Heb. 13:21, all paraphrased,
A Woman's Pilgrimage of Faith, 215

Fragrant Offering

O God, I will be an imitator of You as Your dearly loved child and live a life of love, just as You, Christ, loved me and gave Yourself up for me as a fragrant offering and sacrifice to God. For if I spend myself on behalf of the hungry and satisfy the needs of the oppressed, then my light will rise in the darkness, and my night will become like the noonday. But when I give to the needy, I won't let my left hand know what my right hand is doing, so that my giving may be in secret. Then, Father, You who see what is done in secret will reward me. Now I want to excel also in this gracious ministry of giving. If I serve You, Christ, with this attitude, I will please God.

🌺 PRAYERS, PRAISES, AND PERSONAL NOTES 🌺

_____

_____

_____

_____

_____

Eph. 5:1-2; Isa. 58:10; Matt. 6:3-4; 2 Cor. 8:7b NLT;
Rom. 14:18a NLT, all paraphrased, A Woman's Pilgrimage of Faith, 216

Comfort All Who Mourn

"The Spirit of the Sovereign Lord is on me, because the Lord has anointed me to preach good news to the poor. He has sent me to bind up the brokenhearted, to proclaim freedom for the captives and release from darkness for the prisoners, to proclaim the year of the Lord's favor and the day of vengeance of our God, to comfort all who mourn, and provide for those who grieve in Zion—to bestow on them a crown of beauty instead of ashes, the oil of gladness instead of mourning, and a garment of praise instead of a spirit of despair. They will be called oaks of righteousness, a planting of the Lord for the display of his splendor."

 PRAYERS, PRAISES, AND PERSONAL NOTES

_____

_____

_____

_____

_____

_____

Isa. 61:1-3, A Woman's Pilgrimage of Faith, 217

Be Steadfast

"How beautiful on the mountains are the feet of those who bring good news, who proclaim peace, who bring good tidings, who proclaim salvation." How thankful I am to You, Christ Jesus my Lord, for considering me trustworthy and appointing me to serve You. I need to persevere so that when I have done Your will, O God, I will receive what You have promised. Therefore, as Your beloved one, I will be steadfast, immovable, always abounding in Your work, Lord, knowing that my labor for You is not in vain.

❧ PRAYERS, PRAISES, AND PERSONAL NOTES ❧

_____

_____

_____

_____

_____

_____

_____

Isa. 52:7a not paraphrased; 1 Tim. 1:12 NLT; Heb. 10:36;
1 Cor. 15:58 NKJV paraphrased, A Woman's Pilgrimage of Faith, 218

Faith of Great Worth

O Lord, "I am still not all I should be, but I am focusing all my energies on this one thing: Forgetting the past and looking forward to what lies ahead, I strain to reach the end of the race and receive the prize for which God, through Christ Jesus, is calling us up to heaven." In this I greatly rejoice, though now for a little while I may have had to suffer grief in all kinds of trials. These have come so that my faith—of greater worth than gold, which perishes even though refined by fire—may be proved genuine and may result in praise, glory, and honor when You are revealed, Jesus Christ my Lord.

🌿 PRAYERS, PRAISES, AND PERSONAL NOTES 🌿

_____

_____

_____

_____

_____

_____

Phil. 3:13-14 NLT not paraphrased; 1 Peter 1:5-7 paraphrased,
A Woman's Pilgrimage of Faith, 233

Remember His Benefits

Bless the Lord, O my soul, and do not forget all His benefits—who forgives all my iniquity, who heals all my diseases, who redeems my life from destruction, who crowns me with lovingkindness and tender mercies, who satisfies me with good as long as I live. "Bless the Lord, O my soul: and all that is within me, bless his holy name."

PRAYERS, PRAISES, AND PERSONAL NOTES

_____

_____

_____

_____

_____

_____

_____

_____

_____

Ps. 103:2-3 NRSV; Ps. 103:4 NKJV; Ps. 103:5a NRSV paraphrased;
Ps. 103:1 KJV not paraphrased, A Woman's Pilgrimage of Faith, 233-34

Look to What Is Good

Lord, keep _____ from ever forgetting these words; may they keep them always in mind. May they be careful what they think, because their thoughts run their lives. May they not use their mouths to tell lies and say things that are not true. Help them keep their eyes focused on what is right and look straight ahead to what is good. Strengthen them to be careful what they do and always do what is right. Keep them from turning off the road of goodness; keep them away from evil paths.

PRAYERS, PRAISES, AND PERSONAL NOTES

_____

_____

_____

_____

_____

_____

_____

Prov. 4:21, 23-27 NCV paraphrased

Consider the Days of Old

Lord God, I have considered the days of old, the years of ancient times. I have heard with my ears, O God; our ancestors have told us what work You did in their days, in the times of old. One generation praises Your works to another and declares Your mighty acts. For You are good to all, and Your tender mercies are over all Your works. You have been our dwelling place in all generations. Before the mountains were brought forth or You had formed the earth and the world, even from everlasting to everlasting, You are God.

❧ PRAYERS, PRAISES, AND PERSONAL NOTES ❧

_____

_____

_____

_____

_____

_____

_____

Ps. 77:5; 44:1; 145:4, 9; 90:1-2, all KJV paraphrased

All Nations Shall Serve Him

Yes, all kings shall fall down before You, God; all nations shall serve You. For You shall deliver the needy when they cry—the poor also, and those that have no helper. Lord, You shall spare the poor and needy and shall save the souls of the needy. You shall redeem their souls from deceit and violence, and precious shall their blood be in Your sight. O Lord, Your name shall endure forever; Your name shall be continued as long as the sun, and the people shall be blessed in You; all nations shall call You blessed. Praise be to You, Lord God, the God of Israel, who only does wondrous things. And blessed be Your glorious name forever; let the whole earth be filled with Your glory. Amen and Amen!

❧ PRAYERS, PRAISES, AND PERSONAL NOTES ❧

_____

_____

_____

_____

_____

Ps. 72:11-14, 17-19 KJV paraphrased

Father to the Fatherless

Yes, "let the godly rejoice. Let them be glad in God's presence. Let them be filled with joy. Sing praises to God and to his name! Sing loud praises to him who rides the clouds. His name is the Lord—rejoice in his presence! Father to the fatherless, defender of widows—this is God, whose dwelling is holy. God places the lonely in families; he sets the prisoners free and gives them joy. But for rebels, there is only famine and distress." "The Lord announces victory, and throngs of women shout the happy news." "Praise the Lord; praise God our savior! For each day he carries us in his arms."

✥ PRAYERS, PRAISES, AND PERSONAL NOTES ✥

_____

_____

_____

_____

_____

_____

Ps. 68:3-6, 11, 19 NLT

Rescue the Poor and Helpless

O God, You preside over heaven's court; You pro-nounce judgment on the judges: "'How long will you judges hand down unjust decisions? How long will you shower special favors on the wicked? Give fair judgment to the poor and the orphan; uphold the rights of the oppressed and the destitute. Rescue the poor and help-less; deliver them from the grasp of evil people. But these oppressors know nothing; they are so ignorant! And because they are in darkness, the whole world is shaken to the core.' I say, 'You are gods and children of the Most High. But in death you are mere men. You will fall as any prince, for all must die.' Rise up, O God, and judge the earth, for all the nations belong to you."

✿ PRAYERS, PRAISES, AND PERSONAL NOTES ✿

_____

_____

_____

_____

_____

Ps. 82:1 NLT paraphrased; Ps. 82:2-8 NLT not paraphrased

He Defends the Poor

All-just God, the mountains shall bring peace to the people, and the hills, righteousness. You shall defend the poor among the people. You shall save the children of the needy and shall break in pieces the oppressor. They shall fear You as long as the sun and moon endure, throughout all generations. You shall come down like rain upon the mown grass, as showers that water the earth. In Your days the righteous shall flourish and have abundance of peace so long as the moon endures. You shall have dominion also from sea to sea, and from the river to the ends of the earth. They that dwell in the wilderness shall bow before You, and Your enemies shall lick the dust.

PRAYERS, PRAISES, AND PERSONAL NOTES

_____

_____

_____

_____

_____

Ps. 72:3-9 KJV paraphrased

God's Glory and Majesty

"Praise the Lord! I will thank the Lord with all my heart as I meet with his godly people. How amazing are the deeds of the Lord! All who delight in him should ponder them. Everything he does reveals his glory and majesty. His righteousness never fails. Who can forget the wonders he performs? How gracious and merciful is our Lord! He gives food to those who trust him; he always remembers his covenant." "All he does is just and good, and all his commandments are trustworthy. They are forever true, to be obeyed faithfully and with integrity. He has paid a full ransom for his people. He has guaranteed his covenant with them forever. What a holy, awe-inspiring name he has! Reverence for the Lord is the foundation of true wisdom. The rewards of wisdom come to all who obey him. Praise his name forever!"

PRAYERS, PRAISES, AND PERSONAL NOTES

_____

_____

_____

Ps. 111:1-5, 7-10 NLT not paraphrased

Sing Joyful Songs

Lord, I come and sing to You; I sing joyful songs to the rock of my salvation. I come before Your presence with thanksgiving and sing a joyful song to You with psalms. For, Lord, You are a great God and a great King above all gods. In Your hand are the deep places of the earth; the strength of the hills is Yours also. The sea is Yours, and You made it; and Your hands formed the dry land. Yes, Lord, I come to worship and bow down; I kneel before You, O Lord God, my maker.

PRAYERS, PRAISES, AND PERSONAL NOTES

_____

_____

_____

_____

_____

_____

_____

_____

Ps. 95:1-6 KJV paraphrased

The Lord Reigns

O Lord, You reign; let the earth rejoice; let the multitude of islands be glad. Clouds and darkness are round about You; righteousness and judgment are the habitation of Your throne. Fire goes before You and burns up Your enemies round about. Your lightning lightens the world; the earth sees and trembles. The hills melt like wax at Your presence, Lord, at Your presence, Lord of the whole earth. The heavens declare Your righteousness, and all the people see Your glory. Yes, Lord, You shall reign forever and ever.

PRAYERS, PRAISES, AND PERSONAL NOTES

_____

_____

_____

_____

_____

_____

_____

Ps. 97:1-6; Ex. 15:18, all KJV paraphrased

A Firm Place to Stand

Lord God, set my feet on a rock and give me a firm place to stand on. Help me to show earnestness by trusting in the full assurance of hope until the end, so that I may not be spiritually sluggish, but be an imitator of those who through faith and by practice of patient endurance and waiting inherit the promises. For I need endurance, so that I may do Your will and receive what is promised. Deliver me from drawing back and shrinking in fear, for then You will have no delight or pleasure in me. But may I be among the just and righteous servants who live by faith in You.

PRAYERS, PRAISES, AND PERSONAL NOTES

Ps. 40:2b; Heb. 6:11-12; 10:36, 38b, 38a RSV and AMP, all paraphrased,
A Woman's Walk with God, 38

Apple of God's Eye

We call on You, Lord. Please answer us. Give ear to
_____ and hear their prayers.
Show the wonder of Your great love, You who save by
Your right hand those who take refuge in You from their
foes. It is good to be near You, Lord, and they have made
You their refuge. You are their Shepherd; gather them
as lambs in Your arms, carry them close to Your heart,
and gently lead them. Your eyes are on them because
they fear You; their hope is in Your unfailing love. Keep
them as the apple of Your eye; hide them in the shadow
of Your wings.

PRAYERS, PRAISES, AND PERSONAL NOTES

_____

_____

_____

_____

_____

_____

_____

Ps. 17:6-7; 73:28a; Isa. 40:11; Ps. 33:18; 17:8, all paraphrased

Seek Peace

Ever-forgiving Savior, I repent and turn to You so that my sins may be wiped out, so that times of refreshing may come from You. Each moment of the day help me to turn from evil and do good, to seek peace and pursue it. O Lord, may the fruit of righteousness in my life be peace; may the effect of righteousness be quietness and confidence forever. May I live in a peaceful dwelling place, in a secure home, in an undisturbed place of rest.

🌿 PRAYERS, PRAISES, AND PERSONAL NOTES 🌿

_____

_____

_____

_____

_____

_____

_____

_____

_____

Acts 3:19; Ps. 34:14; Isa. 32:17-18, all paraphrased, A Woman's Walk with God, 21

O How I Love Your Word!

God of grace, I will lift up my hands to Your commandments, which I have loved; and I will meditate on Your statutes. O how I love Your Word! It is my meditation all the day. My soul has kept Your testimonies, and I love them exceedingly. I love Your commandments above gold; yes, above fine gold. Consider how I love Your precepts, and preserve me, O Lord, according to Your lovingkindness.

✺ PRAYERS, PRAISES, AND PERSONAL NOTES ✺

_____

_____

_____

_____

_____

_____

_____

_____

Ps. 119:48, 97, 167, 127, 159, all KJV paraphrased

Promises Fulfilled

Father God, thank You for Your ancient promises that the people walking in darkness would see a great light; on those living in the land of the shadow of death a light would dawn. I praise You for the "shoot" that came up from the stump of Jesse, that from his roots a Branch has borne much fruit. I thank You that the Spirit of the Lord rested on Him—the Spirit of wisdom and of understanding, the Spirit of counsel and of power, the Spirit of knowledge and of the fear of the Lord—and He delighted in the fear of the Lord. Thank You for the star that came out of Jacob, the scepter that rose out of Israel. Praise God, for that "scepter will not depart from Judah, nor the ruler's staff from between his feet, until he comes to whom it belongs and the obedience of the nations is his."

PRAYERS, PRAISES, AND PERSONAL NOTES

_____

_____

_____

_____

Isa. 9:2; 11:1-3a; Num. 24:17b paraphrased; Gen. 49:10 not paraphrased

Mary's Prayer

" 'Oh, how I praise the Lord. How I rejoice in God my Savior! . . . For he, the Mighty One, is holy, and he has done great things for me. His mercy goes on from generation to generation, to all who fear him. His mighty arm does tremendous things! How he scatters the proud and haughty ones! He has taken princes from their thrones and exalted the lowly. He has satisfied the hungry with good things and sent the rich away with empty hands. And how he has helped his servant Israel! He has not forgotten his promise to be merciful.' "

❧ PRAYERS, PRAISES, AND PERSONAL NOTES ❧

_____

_____

_____

_____

_____

_____

_____

Luke 1:46-54 NLT not paraphrased

Immanuel

Lord, You gave a sign: A virgin shall conceive and bear a son and shall call His name Immanuel. For unto us a child is born; unto us a son is given. Yes, Jesus, the government is upon Your shoulders, and Your name is called Wonderful, Counselor, The mighty God, The everlasting Father, The Prince of Peace. Of the increase of Your government and peace there shall be no end, upon the throne of David and upon Your kingdom, to order it and to establish it with judgment and with justice from henceforth even forever. Your zeal, O Lord of hosts, will perform this. Thanks be to God for His unspeakable gift.

✿ PRAYERS, PRAISES, AND PERSONAL NOTES ✿

_____

_____

_____

_____

_____

_____

Isa. 7:14; 9:6-7; 2 Cor. 9:15, all KJV paraphrased

The Lord Is King

"Praise the glory of the Lord's name. Bring an offering and come into his Temple courtyards." "Tell the nations, 'The Lord is king.' The earth is set, and it cannot be moved. He will judge the people fairly. Let the skies rejoice and the earth be glad; let the sea and everything in it shout. Let the fields and everything in them rejoice. Then all the trees of the forest will sing for joy before the Lord, because he is coming. He is coming to judge the world; he will judge the world with fairness and the peoples with truth."

✾ PRAYERS, PRAISES, AND PERSONAL NOTES ✾

_____

_____

_____

_____

_____

_____

_____

Ps. 96:8, 10-13 NCV

Be Self-Controlled

Holy Spirit, strengthen me to prepare my mind for action, to be self-controlled, to set my hope fully on the grace that will be given to me when You, Jesus Christ, are revealed. Help me to be Your obedient child; deliver me from conforming to the evil desires I have now and to the ones I had when I lived in ignorance. But just as You, who have called me, are holy, so I will be holy in all I do; for it is written: "Be holy, because You, Almighty God, are holy."

❧ PRAYERS, PRAISES, AND PERSONAL NOTES ❧

_____

_____

_____

_____

_____

_____

_____

_____

_____

1 Peter 1:13-16 paraphrased, A Woman's Walk with God, 80

Love Others Deeply

O Lord, deliver me from seeking my own good, but let me first seek the good of others. Enable me to devote myself to the service of the saints. Above all, help me to love others deeply, because love covers over a multitude of sins. Teach me how to use the gifts I have received to serve others, faithfully administering Your grace in many different forms. When I speak, may I do so as one speaking the very words of God. When I serve, may I do it with the strength You provide, so that in all things You may be praised through Jesus Christ.

PRAYERS, PRAISES, AND PERSONAL NOTES

_____

_____

_____

_____

_____

_____

_____

1 Cor. 10:24; 16:15b; 1 Peter 4:8, 10-11a, all paraphrased,
A Woman's Walk with God, 170

Bread from Heaven

Jesus, You are the bread of life. My forefathers ate the manna in the desert, and yet they died. You are the bread that came down from heaven, which I may eat and not die. You are the living bread that came down from heaven. I will eat of this bread and will live forever. This bread is Your flesh, which You gave for my life and the life of the world. Jesus, You are the living bread of my life. I come to You, and I will never go hungry. I believe in You, and I will never be thirsty. When Your words come, I will eat them; they are my joy and my heart's delight, for I bear Your name, O Lord God Almighty.

🌿 PRAYERS, PRAISES, AND PERSONAL NOTES 🌿

_____

_____

_____

_____

_____

_____

John 6:48-51, 35; Jer. 15:16, all paraphrased, A Woman's Walk with God, *126*

Love and Faithfulness

O Holy Lord, "Do not those who plot evil go astray? But those who plan what is good find love and faithfulness." For love and truth bring forgiveness of sin. By respecting You, Lord, I pray _____ will avoid evil. Let love and faithfulness never leave them. Don't ever let them forget kindness and truth. May they wear these virtues like necklaces. Write them on their hearts as if on tablets. For love and faithfulness will keep them safe. For all Your ways, O Lord, are loving and faithful for those who keep the demands of Your covenant.

✺ PRAYERS, PRAISES, AND PERSONAL NOTES ✺

_____

_____

_____

_____

_____

_____

Prov. 14:22 not paraphrased; Prov. 16:6 NCV; Prov. 3:3a; Prov. 3:3 NCV;
Prov. 20:28a; Ps. 25:10 paraphrased

New Heavens and New Earth

Ever-living Lord, You said, "Behold, I will create new heavens and a new earth. The former things will not be remembered, nor will they come to mind." "Past troubles will be forgotten and hidden from my eyes." I will surely forget my trouble, recalling it only as waters gone by. I will not call to mind the former things or ponder things of the past. O Lord, You will do something new; now it will spring forth.

❧ PRAYERS, PRAISES, AND PERSONAL NOTES ❧

_____

_____

_____

_____

_____

_____

_____

_____

_____

Isa. 65:17, 16b not paraphrased; Job 11:16; Isa. 43:18-19a NAS95 paraphrased,
A Woman's Pilgrimage of Faith, 227

Visit A Woman's Walk website at: womanswalk.com
Featuring *Prayer for the Day, A Woman's Walk* newsletter, and a free copy of *The Book of John: Bible Study Quicknotes for Busy People* by seniors' pastor Darrell Tesdall.

Or contact us at: sheilacragg@womanswalk.com

Title Index